THE YACHTSMAN'S LAWYER

EDMUND WHELAN
Barrister at Law

First published 1989
Revised 1993

CONTENTS

CHAPTER 1

YACHT OWNERSHIP AND REGISTRATION

Because of the historical importance of shipping to the U.K., the legal concept of the ownership of a vessel, and the mechanism of recording this, has developed differently to the law of ownership of objects or 'chattels' in general.

English law developed as a pragmatic system and has never had a separate theory of ownership. The notion of ownership is perhaps best explained as the sum total of the powers of use and disposal of an object which are allowed by law. Ownership of a 'thing' (such as a yacht) includes the absolute right to sell it and the right to enjoy quiet and uninterrupted possession of it.

Because merchant ships are large, movable and valuable assets and because their use involves potentially immense liabilities to others it is internationally recognised that they should each have a national identity so that rights and obligations can be identified and regulated, hence the notion of a 'British Ship'.

At one end of the scale of size, ownership and use of a merchant ship involves compliance with a number of complex statutory requirements. At the other, ownership of a small dinghy involves virtually none - although continued vigilance and effort may be needed if this absence of restrictions is to remain. Yachts can generally be owned and used in U.K. waters without any special formalities, although many owners choose to register their boats voluntarily.

Under Merchant Shipping law, the concept of ownership is inextricably linked with the requirement of registration. The Merchant Shipping Act 1894 made it a requirement that all British ships over 15 Register Tons used otherwise than solely on the rivers or coastal waters of the UK should be registered.

There was however no penalty for failure to register: the consequences were that the owner did not get the benefits of British ownership when overseas.

The Merchant Shipping Act 1988 changed the emphasis. The requirement to register was removed and the classes of person entitled to register a British Ship were widened.

For the purpose of the Merchant Shipping Acts, "ships" are defined as all vessels 'used in navigation not propelled by oars'. This wide definition therefore includes small pleasure craft such as motorised inflatables and single-handed dinghies. Recent High Court cases leave the status of very small craft such as jetskis and windsurfers open to doubt. In France such craft have been classified as "beach toys" (engins de plage) for many years, and a similar opinion appears to be emerging in the United Kingdom.

BRITISH SHIPS AND THEIR REGISTRATION

There are complex statutory rules defining
- which ships are to be regarded as British
- who can own a British ship
- the forms of registration and how it is effected.

As far as most yachts are concerned, the relevant rules are these:

1. It is not necessary to register a yacht used only in UK waters.
2. A yacht is eligible for registration, provided she is British owned.
   Registration may be effected either under Part 1 Merchant Shipping Act 1894 (from now on referred to as 'Part 1') or under the Merchant Shipping Act 1983 (which made provision for the Small Ships Register now administered by the Driver and Vehicle Licensing Agency on behalf of the Department of Transport).
3. A yacht may be owned by either one or a number of persons. If she has been registered under the Part 1 procedure then her legal ownership is notionally divided into 64 parts, or shares. A sole owner will have all 64 shares; multiple ownership involves dividing up these shares into the desired proportion. Thus 32: 32 for a boat owned in equal half shares; 16:16:16:16:16 for a syndicate of 4, and so on.
   Shares in a yacht may also be held in unequal proportions and indeed the concept of a majority shareholding is particularly relevant following the extension of the right of part- ownership in a British ship to foreign nationals (Merchant Shipping Act 1988)
4. A yacht is automatically British if she is either:
   - registered (either Part 1 or SSR) or
   - not registered
     - but less than 24 metres in length and
     - wholly owned by one or more persons qualified to own a British Ship.

   The main categories of persons who are so qualified are:
   - British Citizens
   - various other categories of British Subject listed in the 1988 Act
   - Citizens of the Republic of Ireland resident in the United Kingdom
   - companies registered in the UK or in certain overseas territories.

- EC nationals resident in the UK by special arrangement with the Registrar General of British Shipping.

The most obvious privilege to which a British Ship is entitled is the right to wear the British Ensign.

THE SMALL SHIPS REGISTER

Since 1983 it has been possible as an alternative to full Part 1 registration to enter a vessel on the Small Ships Register at present administered by the Driver and Vehicle Licensing Agency.

The law relating to the SSR is contained in the Merchant Shipping Act 1983 and the Merchant Shipping (Small Ships Register) Regulations (1983 S.1. 1983/1470).

The procedure, which is designed to be as simple and inexpensive as possible, was bought into effect to provide an easy means of acquiring documentary evidence of the nationality of the ship-primarily to enable British boat owners going overseas to comply with foreign regulations.

Entry on the SSR also enables an owner to fulfil the registration condition for the grant of a permit to wear a privileged ensign (when the owner is a member of a privileged club) and also enables bonded stores to be shipped out of the country on voyages beyond the designated limits.

For a yacht to be registered she must be:

- less than 24 metres in length
- owned by a person who is a Commonwealth or Irish Citizen resident in the UK (if two or more persons own the vessel they must all fulfil this condition), or by an EC national resident in the UK by special arrangement with the Registrar General of Shipping.
- not registered under Part 1 Merchant Shipping Act 1894

These straightforward conditions enable the great majority of owners to register without any problems. One of the effects of the regulations is however that British owners who live permanently abroad are ineligible. If they wish to register their boat they must use the full Part 1 procedure, for which there is no residence qualification.

It should also be noted that only individuals may enter a boat on the SSR. Company owned vessels must use the full procedure.

The following additional points should be noted:

- Marine mortgages cannot be recorded against the SSR (if a lender requires this security the vessel must be Part 1 registered)
- SSR is not (unlike the Part 1 Register) a register of title to the vessel. In this respect it is somewhat similar to the log-book of a car, which simply records the 'keeper'

of the vehicle.
- fishing vessels or submersibles cannot be entered on the SSR

To enter a boat on the SSR, send for an application form and guidance notes to:

The Small Ships Register
DVLA
Swansea
SA99 1BX 0792 783355

The registered owner is required to mark the vessel so as to identify her with the Certificate issued on registration. This is done by displaying the letters "SSR" followed by the issued number on an exterior visible surface of the craft, in the way explained in the guidance notes. Professionally made plates can be supplied by the Royal Yachting Association if requested.

The fee for a five year registration is £10.00, after which it is renewable. If the boat changes ownership, registration is renewable immediately.

PART 1 REGISTRATION

Part 1 Registration is the only option available if:
- the owner wishes to register and the vessel is over 24 metres in length

or – the vessel is owned by a company registered in the UK

or – a person or company lending money on the security of the vessel requires a marine mortgage to be registered against it.

Other yachts can be Part 1 registered if their owners prefer, provided adequate title to the vessel can be shown.

NATIONALITY AND RESIDENCE QUALIFICATIONS FOR PART 1 REGISTRATION

The 1988 Merchant Shipping Act has widened the qualifying categories and these are now considerably more complex than previously.

Prior to the 1988 Act, the main categories of persons qualified to register were British Citizens and companies registered either in the UK or in defined overseas territories. There was no residence qualification for individuals.

The 1988 Act extends the qualification to Irish citizens who are resident in the UK and also provides that a foreign person (i.e. neither British, Irish or a UK company) may own a minority interest (less than 32/64) shares in a British ship. There are detailed rules regulating the conditions under which part foreign ownership may be registered, based on the appointment of a 'representative person' in the UK. Yacht owners wishing to take advantage of these provisions in the Act should refer to the Act and/or take further advice.

Despite this statutory concession, foreigners who are resident in the U.K. and who wholly own, or have a majority share in, a vessel they wish to register are still not admissible to entry on either of the registers, according to the Act, despite the U.K.'s membership of the EC. This is because registration is a recognition of the nationality rather than the place of residence of the owner. Overseas nationals resident in the U.K. should (unless wishing to register through a company) approach their own national registration authorities.

However, in the Factortame II case (1991) C-246/89 it was held by the European Court that the nationality requirements laid down in the 1988 Act infringed the Treaty of Rome, which prohibits discrimination between nationals of Member States on the grounds of nationality. Therefore although the 1988 Act is still the relevant statute, it has been ruled unlawful by the European Court, and the Registrar General of Shipping has made special provision for EC nationals resident in the UK, until such a time as new legislation is passed to reflect the Factortame II judgment.

So far as non-EC nationals are concerned, an unqualified person may wish to consider placing the vessel in the name of, say, a British citizen in order to effect a British registration. It should be realised however that Section 9 of the 1894 Act requires an applicant to make a declaration which includes the statement that "... no unqualified person or body of persons is entitled as owner to any legal or beneficial share in the ship or any share therein".

The distinction between legal and beneficial ownership is discussed at the end of this chapter.

PROCEDURE FOR PART 1 REGISTRATION

Part 1 registration requires a formal measurement procedure which, for ships under 45 ft (13.7 metres) LOA, can be undertaken in a simplified form by RYA measurers at a reduced fee. Even so Part 1 registration, which involves provision of full documentary evidence of title for scrutiny by the registrar, as well as the services of a professional surveyor, will leave little change out of £350.00.

Details of tonnage measurement of vessels under 45 feet are given in Merchant Shipping Notice M1162, available from the RYA.

Where a yacht already on the Register changes hands the fee for amending the ownership particulars on the register is £80.00. A purchaser of a second-hand Part 1 registered yacht may be tempted to opt for the cheaper alternative of "closing" the Part 1 registration and re-registering on the SSR. He should bear in mind, however, that the initial saving of £70.00 may prove to be expensive, as the SSR fee is payable every five years and the initial fee for transfer will probably be more than recouped when the new owner comes to sell. A prospective purchaser will appreciate the advantage of evidence of title being available by virtue of the Part 1 registration, as well as the ability to register a marine mortgage which may be necessary for subsequent purchasers.

The situation often arises where a purchaser of a yacht who has been careless in investigating the seller's documents of title finds that his yacht is registered in the name of a previous owner who cannot be traced, or who has not completed a Bill of Sale properly, or who, having been traced, refuses to sign a correctly completed Bill of Sale or will only do so under unreasonable conditions (e.g. demanding a fee). Unfortunately, in these circumstances, there is nothing the new owner can do to force the previous owner to provide him with a Bill of Sale or such other documents as are necessary. It may be necessary to approach a solicitor, experienced in marine registration procedure, for an application to be made to the High Court (Admiralty Division) to direct the Registrar of British Shipping to amend the record. This can be an expensive and time-consuming procedure and prospective purchasers of yachts registered on the Part 1 Register can avoid this by making the necessary investigations as to title (i.e. legal ownership) before they part with their money, even though they may be quite satisfied as to beneficial ownership.

Another problem frequently confronting owners of old yachts which have not previously been registered is that there is insufficient documentation to trace ownership back to the time when the yacht was built. This frequently happens where a yacht has changed hands on a number of occasions without formal Bills of Sale or even written contracts. The Registrar of British Shipping will not accept an application for registration without full documentation being available. However, under the terms of the Merchant Shipping Act 1894 he is entitled to take into account "other adequate evidence" and in these circumstances a statutory declaration of ownership, supported by an affidavit as to the reasons why certain documentary evidence is missing will normally be sufficient to satisfy the Registrar. Unfortunately this procedure can only apply to new registrations and is not applicable where an existing registration is to be transferred into the name of a new owner.

THE DIFFERENT WAYS IN WHICH A BOAT MAY BE OWNED

If an individual person purchases a boat for his own use he becomes the sole legal owner of it. This is the simplest form of ownership, as beneficial ownership and legal title are kept together.

If two or more persons buy a boat together (each joining in the contract with the seller) they will, if they do nothing else, become joint legal owners of it. They have, as between each other "unity of title" and no "distinction of interest".

An important consequence of joint ownership is the right of survivorship. This means that if one of the joint owners dies, his legal title in the vessel passes automatically (and irrespective of the contents of a will) to the surviving joint owner(s). This may be desirable in the case of a husband and wife team but is unlikely to be what a group of friends owning a boat together would want. In such a case the beneficiaries of the deceased's estate would obviously be entitled to a share in the proceeds of the vessel, but the legal title would need to be transferred separately to them by the surviving joint owners.

To avoid this difficulty, it would be more appropriate for those buying a vessel in partnership to become part-owners (or strictly speaking co-owners). Each would then own a distinct legal share in the vessel.

There is no strict need for a complicated legal document to record the shares owned by such a group, but the RYA does provide for members a draft form of agreement for the syndicate ownership of a yacht. As well as providing sufficient evidence of the fact of co-ownership this also deals with the practical management aspects of syndicate ownership. This form of agreement is reproduced in Appendix (5)

If, say, two friends or an unmarried partnership buy a boat together and do not want the rule of survivorship to apply it would be sensible to make a short written declaration (preferably professionally witnessed) setting out their respective interests in the craft.

The beginning of this chapter mentioned the concept of the division of the interests in the ship into 64 notional parts. This has its origins in merchant shipping practice. For the purpose of the present discussion we need only say that if two or more persons register a vessel under the Part 1 procedure, the fact of such an allocation of shares in her will be sufficient evidence of the existence of co-ownership.

Everything said so far applies only to what is known as the "legal" ownership in a vessel. A person or persons who are such legal owners will appear to the outside world from the ship's papers (and the entry on the Register, if any) as if they were the only persons with an interest in her. They will in fact be the only person(s) entitled to deal with the vessel (eg. sell or mortgage it). They may however not be the persons who "own" the craft in the colloquial sense. Thus, for example, a large syndicate - perhaps several hundred people - may have contributed informal shares towards the purchase and running of a large vessel and have appointed a single person to hold formal title on behalf of all of them; or several friends may have all contributed towards the boat but are content for her to be registered in one name only; or perhaps the members of a yacht club may decide to purchase a vessel for club use and will place her in the names of the Trustees appointed under the club's constitution (in the case of an unincorporated club they must do this, as such a club's property can only effectively be held by Trustees). In all these examples the group of people who have in actuality the benefit of the use of the vessel are the beneficial owners and the person(s) who hold formal title to her are the legal owner(s). Legal and beneficial ownership can, and in most cases do, coincide. Thus the person described at the opening of this section who went out and bought a boat for himself is both the legal and the beneficial owner of her.

CHAPTER 2

BUYING AND SELLING A YACHT

Although a yacht may be equivalent to a large detached house both in size and value, the purchase of a yacht may be as simple as the purchase of a bicycle. In the case of an unregistered yacht at least, no special form of contract is required and no particular transfer mechanism can be demanded. In Behnke -v- Bede Shipping Company (1927) 1KB 649 it was confirmed that ships (and that term is defined as any vessel used in navigation not propelled by oars) are chattels within the meaning of what is now Section 61 of the Sale of Goods Acts 1979 (the consolidating Act for all previous relevant legislation). In all cases the sale of a yacht in this country is subject to the Act except where the yacht in question is registered under the provisions of the 1894 Merchant Shipping Act, Section 24 of which provides that the property in the ship passes only on the transfer of a Bill of Sale from the seller to the buyer. However, as with the purchase of any chattel, the Act will only be relevant where there is an enforceable contract for the sale, and it is the terms of the agreement that are of fundamental importance.

Even although you are buying from (or selling to) someone you know you can trust, you are very strongly advised to enter into a written agreement along the lines of one of the standard forms available. The RYA provides a draft agreement for the sale of a second hand yacht between private persons. This is reproduced at Appendix 3.

AGREEMENT FOR SALE

The general legal distinctions between a sale (whereby the property in the goods is transferred from seller to buyer) and an agreement for sale (which operates simply as a mutually binding promise to sell on the happening of some future conveyance or condition) applies to yachts as to other chattels. A binding agreement to sell may arise from a simple conversation, so long as the parties have agreed on the subject matter and the price and have agreed to be bound by the offer and acceptance of a price. While it will always make sense to require a written form of contract to define and record the rights and liabilities of the parties, verbal contracts are frequently entered into with the result that, should a change of heart or circumstance arise, recollections as to precisely what was said and agreed will differ between the parties. The point of dispute most frequently raised between the parties is whether an enforceable contract has come into effect at all. In the case of Lovegrove -v- Campbell (1948) 82 LL Rep 615 a dispute arose as to whether there had been a firm offer and acceptance so as to form the sound basis of a contract. A prospective buyer offered to buy a yacht. The owners replied that they were "a little undecided" as to that offer but later accepted it. The buyer then retracted the offer. The Court held that, since there was no clear recovation of the buyer's offer prior to acceptance by the owners, and the offer had been accepted within a reasonable time, a binding contract had been made between the parties and the buyer was liable in damages.

The fact that the agreement remains conditional (i.e. subject to survey, or subject to satisfactory sea trials) will not of itself mean that a binding contract does not exist. In the case of The Merak (1976) 2Ll 250 the owners of the vessel agreed a price for her sale with the purchasers subject to inspection by the buyer at a port and date to be agreed. A form of standard contract was agreed to. The owners then failed to make the vessel available for inspection, but the Court of Appeal held that a binding contract had been concluded and accordingly the owners were in breach of contract.

TERMS OF THE AGREEMENT

The terms of a contract may be either express or implied and may be construed as either conditions or warranties.

A condition is defined as a term that goes to the heart of the contract, the remedy for breach of which is rescission (the right to reject the goods and require a refund of purchase price); a warranty is a less important term, breach of which is remediable but which will still give the buyer the right to claim damages.

MISREPRESENTATIONS

A buyer who has entered into a contract on the strength of a misrepresentation has the choice of treating a breach of condition as a breach of warranty, keeping the goods and making a claim for damages. If he wishes to reject the goods and claim the return of the price, he must not delay before exercising this right.

Where a private seller is negotiating with a private buyer for the sale of a yacht, he will usually make a number of representations which may become terms of the contract (either as conditions or warranties) as to the design, construction, history, characteristics and condition of the yacht. Where these representations can be shown to be false in some way, and the buyer can show that they were instrumental in inducing him to enter into the contract, he will be entitled to rescission of the contract or damages. The legal rules which determine the remedy available to a purchaser who has suffered a misrepresentation are rather complex but basically:

- if the misrepresentation is serious enough to amount to a breach of condition, he will be entitled to rescind the contract, return the goods (if possession has passed) and claim a refund of the price, (but he must not delay in doing so).
- if the misrepresentation is less serious and can be treated only as a breach of warranty, his remedy is a cash adjustment (damages).
- a purchaser who has suffered a breach of condition may choose to keep the goods and claim damages, rather than return them.
- The detail of these rules also varies depending on whether a misrepresentation has been made innocently, negligently or fraudulently.

In interpreting the conduct of the parties in the course of negotiations, the court will have regard as much to the intention of the parties (in the context of normal business practice) as to the strict rules of offer and acceptance.

RYA STANDARD FORM AGREEMENT

Unless the parties have taken the precaution of drawing up an agreed written contract before the agreement is fixed orally, they will find, in the event of a subsequent disagreement reaching the court, that rules of interpretation of contracts will be imposed. To avoid the need for an incomplete oral agreement being subjected to expensive and time-consuming legal proceedings, it makes sense to use a tried and tested form of written contract. One such standard form which provides a fair balance between the interests of the buyer and the interests of the seller is that published by the RYA and reproduced at Appendix 3. Where a broker is involved he will usually prevail on the parties to rely on the YBDSA/ABYA agreement which contains the same major provisions.

The RYA agreement provides that a deposit of 10% of the agreed price shall be paid on the signing of the agreement, and that the contract shall be subject to the purchaser's right to have the yacht surveyed at his own cost within a specified period. In the event of material defects or deficiencies being found that had not previously been notified to the purchaser in writing, he then has the option,(which must be exercised within 14 days of the survey) of rejecting the yacht and cancelling the agreement, or requiring the purchaser either to reduce the agreed price or to make good the defects, at his own expense and without delay, to the satisfaction of the purchaser's surveyor. If the vendor does not accept these conditions within 21 days then the agreement is deemed to be rescinded.

The survey may not be taken simply as an opportunity for the purchaser to change his mind about his proposed purchase;

whether a defect or deficiency is "material" leaves much scope for professional argument, but in general terms a defect will not be material if it can be properly described as trivial or minimal, or requiring remedial action the cost of which is insignificant in relation to the value of the vessel as a whole. Thus a small scratch in the topsides, a frayed wire or rope, a burnt-out navigation light bulb or broken crockery, or even a combination of all these defects, will be regarded as trivial. On the other hand sloppy rudder bearings, low engine compression, worn out sails, or numerous deep gelcoat chips that had not been apparent on initial inspection could be regarded as material defects even if not serious.

The standard form agreement provides for the yacht to be accepted by the purchaser either 14 days from the signing of the agreement or, if a survey has been carried out, 15 days after the survey or, if remedial works were required, upon the vendor notifying the purchaser in writing that the works have been completed, or upon a mutual agreement to reduce the price following a survey.

Upon the acceptance of the yacht by the purchaser, the 10% deposit becomes a part payment of the purchase price, the balance being payable within 7 days. At the same time the risk in the yacht also passes to the purchaser, although the property in the yacht does not pass to the purchaser until the balance of the price has been paid. It is important to ascertain which of the parties bears the risk in the case, for example, of a delivery voyage (or a delivery by road transport). In Ambler -v- Graves-Tage (1930) 36 Ll Rep. 145 a yacht being delivered from Bridlington to Whitstable was destroyed by fire. The yacht was insured for a greater sum than the purchase price and a dispute arose as to whether the buyer was entitled merely to the return of the purchase price or to the full insurance money. In the event it was held that the risk in the vessel had passed to the buyer and he was entitled to the full insurance payment.

BUYING ABROAD (NON EC TERRITORY)

Cheap air travel and a proliferation of cheap marina berths in the Mediterranean have led to thousands of British yachts being bought, moored and sold in Mediterranean countries. The standard form contract contains provisions to reduce the risk involved in buying a yacht overseas. By Clause 3.2 the vendor warrants that "the craft has been properly .... imported into (the country in question) and that all appropriate local taxes and dues have been paid and that the proposed sale is in accordance with all relevant local laws and regulations". While overseas regulations are dealt with more fully later, the position of temporarily or permanently imported yachts is of significance here. Most members of the

Customs Union (a wider body than the European Community) will permit Customs Union nationals tax free temporary importation rights for yachts.

BUYING ABROAD (EC TERRITORY)

Since 1st January 1993 the EC has become a single financial area in the context of VAT payments and the import and export of yachts. The rule now is that once a yacht has had VAT paid on her in any EC State (and not refunded or reclaimed) she may then be bought and sold, and used, without any restriction in any other EC State. Although this means a reduction in bureaucracy in some ways, and the end of the old 6 month rule applied by most EC States, it also creates difficulties for owners of yachts without proof of VAT payment. For a yacht owner who has the original receipted VAT invoice from the builder or supplier among his ship's papers, there is no problem. He will be able to respond to spot checks by the UK or overseas Customs officials, and satisfy the questions of a potential buyer without difficulty. An owner without proof of VAT payment may however find himself having to meet a VAT demand at any time and in any place in the EC if he is subjected to a spot check unless he can prove:-

either

(i) that the yacht was built before 31st December 1984 (i.e. was more than 8 years old on 31st December 1992)

and

(ii)that the yacht was in EC territory on 31st December 1992/1st January 1993

or

that the amount of VAT to be collected is negligible (which in the UK is interpreted as meaning that the yacht is valued at less than £4000).

In some cases, where an owner can collate sufficient circumstantial evidence to show that VAT was paid, he may be able to obtain from HM Customs a Single Administrative Document certifying that the yacht is not liable to VAT. Application forms and other detailed notes on the SAD procedure are available from the RYA. The SAD certificate would also be useful for any craft complying with (i) and (ii) above as providing a single, authoritative, standard certificate, rather than a bundle of papers that may be incomprehensible to an overseas Customs official.

The significance of these new arrangements to the prospective buyer of a yacht whether in the UK or elsewhere in the EC is that he should satisfy himself absolutely as to the yacht's VAT status, or prepare himself for a substantial VAT liability. In some cases the absence of VAT records may be grounds for a buyer to re-negotiate the price to be paid, or to obtain a binding indemnity from the seller against the possible liability.

BUYING THROUGH A BROKER

The Boating Industry Code of Practice (compiled jointly by the British Marine Industries Federation, the Association of Brokers and Yacht Agents, The Yacht Brokers, Designers and Surveyors Association, and The Yacht Harbours Association) lays down certain stipulations for the members of these bodies.

Section 4 of the Code provides that brokers should include in their terms of business :-

(i) An undertaking by the Vendor that he has power to dispose of the vessel with the concurrence of joint owners, of a mortgagee or a hire purchase company; that defects have been declared and that there is indemnity in respect of misrepresentations covered by the 1976 Act.

(ii) That the broker should ensure that information given to a purchaser is accurate and has pointed out defects known to the seller.

The Code then deals with the broker's obligations to the vendor regarding offers made and how the sale price should be quoted.

It also recommends the use of a Sale and Purchase Agreement for a Secondhand Yacht as approved by the Association of Brokers and Yacht Agents and if that is not used then, at least, any deposit paid by a purchaser should be deemed and stated to be subject to the terms of that Agreement.

As to any Particulars of Sale, the Code of Practice suggests that the purchaser should be warned to check them himself, and to employ a qualified marine surveyor to carry out a full survey. Prospective purchasers are also to be advised to have an engine trial conducted.

Quite obviously, a cursory look at the outside of an engine is hardly the way to ensure that it is in working order and if the value of the engine is substantial it is usual for a qualified engineer to be commissioned to examine the engine, leaving the surveyor to check everything else on the vessel.

As to survey, the Code specifically states that a broker should not advise a purchaser not to have a survey. In fact, the clause suggests that the broker should make sure that such a survey is entirely independent in that the surveyor should have no connection with the seller or the seller's broker, although there is no reason why the seller's agent should not recommend a surveyor if requested to do so by the buyer. This seems a very proper precaution to protect the purchaser and the broker from any difficulties which may arise between them.

The Code also recommends brokers to keep sale proceeds (including deposits and part payments) in a separate banking account much as solicitors keep client's money entirely separate from their own practice account. Again, a sensible recommendation to protect the vendor's money in the case of the broker's insolvency. This is followed by a procedure for exchange of documents and purchase money, a completion date, procedure for delivery etc.

Two matters that are not referred to in either the ABYA standard form agreement or in the Code are the treatment of the purchase money in the period between completion and final re-registration (in the case of a yacht on the Part I Register) and the physical accessibility of the yacht to the water after completion.

From the purchaser's point of view it should be an express term of the contract that the broker should not release the purchase money to the seller until, at the very least, the seller has delivered to the broker the Registration Document, signed Bill of Sale and any relevant mortgage release documents. In the case of an overseas seller or one who is unlikely to have any assets within the jurisdiction of the British Courts after the sale is complete, it would be sensible to insist that the broker retains the proceeds until re-registration formalities are complete.

A frequent problem facing buyers coming to take delivery of a yacht on hard standing is that between the initial viewing and the day of final completion, particularly in the laying-up season, the yacht may have become totally blocked-in. This can necessitate waiting until the spring or paying for the labour involved in re-shuffling all the yachts on the way to the boatyard slip or crane. An express term written into the agreement that the seller or broker/ boatyard will ensure accessibility to the dockside or roadway will avoid any unplanned additional expense.

BUYING PRIVATELY

Although buying through a broker provides no guarantee that the seller is the bona fide owner, and that there are no undisclosed mortgages or other charges on the yacht, most brokers are concerned enough to preserve their professional reputation to satisfy themselves that the seller is genuine, and can normally be expected to detect a potential fraud.

Those buying direct from a private seller, without a broker being involved, would be well advised to carry out their own investigations as to title. In the case of a yacht on the Part 1 Register, this should be done by contacting the Registrar at the Port of Registry.

This will reveal:-

– the names(s) of the present registered owner (which obviously should be the seller and previous owners)

– whether the vessel is subject to any marine mortgages (in which case detailed arrangements must be made for their discharge at the time of sale).

A change of ownership of a registered vessel takes effect from the delivery of the completed bill of sale to the buyer. Unlike practice in the Land Registry (which deals with title to land and houses) it is not possible to "reserve" a clear title by making a search in the Register which confers priority for a set period of time. It is for this reason, and to avoid the possibility of fraud, at least in the case of purchase or mortgage of large vessels, that the parties or their representatives normally attend at the Registrar's office to sign and immediately present the document to the Registrar. Thus transfer and re-registration are simultaneous with the handing over of the cash or banker's draft payment.

In the case of an unregistered yacht the prospective purchaser should check the vendor's title by asking for documentary evidence of ownership from the time the yacht was built (by reference to the Builder's Certificate and subsequent contracts and/or Bills of Sale, which should be kept in the yacht's file).

Very often no documentation exists, or the seller may attempt to rely on a Small Ships Registration Certificate or an old International Certificate for Pleasure Navigation. Neither of these is true evidence of ownership or title. In such a case a prospective purchaser can do no more than try to establish the bona fides of the seller himself, ask for a sight of marina or moorings receipts or insurance policies in the seller's name going back a few years, and ask questions at the marina harbour master's office. The buyer should also extract a written contractual undertaking that the seller has the right to pass good title (free of charges, liens, other interests etc.) and that he will indemnify the purchaser against any undisclosed obligations or encumbrances coming to light after the sale. Section 12 of the Sale of Goods Act 1979 implies such a condition into every contract for the sale of goods in any case, but it is comforting and avoids ambiguity to have it in writing as well. An undertaking to this effect is included in the RYA standard contract referred to above.

With a number of leading finance houses now lending substantial sums of money on unregistered craft, there is no means by which a buyer can be sure that an unregistered yacht is not subject to a mortgage. In the case of The Shizelle (1991) the High Court held that a mortgage on an unregistered yacht was binding against a bona fide third party purchaser, and he had the yacht repossessed from him by the finance company when the seller, who had fraudulently retained the proceeds of the sale and had not paid off the mortgage, defaulted on his instalments. A sensible precaution in circumstances where the seller is not personally known to the buyer is to check with the major finance companies, giving the name and address of the seller and the name and description of the yacht. Although no check can ever be comprehensive, the marine finance market in the UK tends to be very centralised, and a check with the six leading companies will cover at least 95% of lending sources.

The RYA has been campaigning for the establishment of a central record of unregistered mortgages, but at the time of writing, the finance companies as a whole have been unwilling to agree to the setting up of such a system.

SURVEYS

We cannot stress too strongly that to purchase a secondhand yacht without the benefit of at least a hull condition survey is a false economy. Even in the case of a comparatively new GRP yacht there is much that can be wrong, and indeed horror stories abound of osmosis, soft patches, gel coat flaking, and delamination even on yachts of less than 12 months old which may still be cosmetically perfect, but nevertheless suffer from serious structural problems. It is very important for the buyer to take responsibility for instructing his own surveyor rather than leaving it to the vendor's broker to make the arrangements.

The Yacht Brokers, Designers and Surveyors Association has in membership a number of competent surveyors in all regions who may be called upon and who are required to maintain professional indemnity insurance.

A full survey is both time consuming and very expensive. Both the time and the money might well be justified in the case of the purchase of one boat but what is the situation if the survey is so bad that the buyer decides not to buy his first choice? He may go on surveying one boat after another until he finds that he has insufficient funds actually to buy a boat.

Therefore, we would suggest that the answer, initially, is to commission a "preliminary" survey on a boat which he may wish to buy. This will at least eliminate the really "dud" boat which may look attractive but which a professional can immediately see is not worth purchasing. A buyer should never expect the surveyor to value a boat. This is not the purpose of his inspection unless specifically invited to do so and, even then, any statement which he may make will clearly only be an expression of his personal opinion.

It is always worthwhile being with the surveyor when he makes his survey. He will only write down what is defective and will only be heard to say what is good. Expense may also be minimised by assisting him to remove bits and pieces so that he can make a proper inspection. Even when a surveyor is asked to make a complete survey, unless he strips the engine down, he cannot and does not survey the engine. After all, what can he really tell about an engine even if it has been run for a few minutes ? Unscrupulous sellers have ways of making a worn engine run sweetly for a few hours.

Since the engine is almost invariably a most expensive item to repair, and since a surveyor does not normally inspect an engine, it is best to employ a mechanic for that purpose. A qualified person can, by testing compression ratios etc., by visual inspection and by running the engine for a period tell a great deal about its condition.

LLOYDS SURVEYS

Immediately the word "Lloyds" is mentioned, most people (quite properly) expect "excellence". If the yacht was originally built under Lloyds supervision she can be surveyed by Lloyds.

There are various levels of Lloyds supervision.

The expression "Registered at Lloyds" has no connotations other than the fact that the boat has been voluntarily entered in the Lloyds Register of Yachts. This publication is entirely independent from the well-known insurance corporation. If however, an owner can produce a currently valid Lloyds Certificate then, whilst it may not be perfect, the boat has some standing.

Many GRP boats may have a certificate which states that the hull was moulded under Lloyds Approved Conditions. This means that a Lloyds surveyor inspected the hull maker's premises and labour force and judged them to be suitable for the production of good quality boats at the time of inspection.

The boat may have a Hull Moulding Certificate or a Hull Construction Certificate. These indicate that a surveyor inspected and was satisfied with this particular hull at the time of building. It must be noted that this refers to the hull only, and carries no guarantee in respect of the rig, engine installation, skin fittings etc.

Better still is the "Lloyds Register Building Certificate". This means that the hull was passed as satisfactory, as was the machinery, electrical installations, shafting, propeller, stern gland and stern gear, pumping and piping gear, fire fighting equipment and steering gear and all were fitted under supervision and to Lloyds requirements at the time of building.

Note that all the inspections mentioned above were done at the time of building and there is no continuing guarantee.

There are, however, two "continuing" classifications by Lloyds.

100A which shows that the boat not only was constructed to the satisfaction of a Lloyds surveyor but has been maintained to those standards.

100AI indicates that, in addition, the anchors, cables and warps meet with the approval of Lloyds.

These classifications have to be reviewed every two years and are only granted after a thorough survey, the cost of which is considerable. After every four years, the survey is a specially stringent one.

However, even these classifications are not absolute guarantees because, if an owner has not reported any occurrence which may affect the structure of a craft which has been classified, then the classification lapses. In effect, you could buy a yacht with these classifications which only a few weeks before has been run aground. If this event has not been reported, the yacht would be "unclassified".

Finally, and perhaps most importantly, we repeat that however a survey has been carried out it will be difficult and time consuming to secure any compensation from the surveyor in the event of subsequent failures. Statements made are upon the condition of the yacht at the time of the survey, and where defects subsequently come to light, it will be up to the owner to prove that the surveyor should have noticed the defects if he is to succeed in a claim for compensation.

CONSTRUCTION OF A NEW CRAFT

So far as the purchase of a new yacht is concerned, some years ago the RYA agreed with the British Marine Industries Federation the terms of a standard form agreement for the construction of a new craft or completion from a bare hull to the customer's order.

What could not be agreed was that all sellers of such craft would use the agreement. The full text of the standard form agreement is set out at Appendix (1). Its conditions deal with the majority of the pitfalls likely to occur.

Although it is of course up to the client and builder to come to agreement on terms for payment, and in each case these terms are open to negotiation, some code is called for in respect of payment of the full price. A "normal" pricing schedule would be a 5 or 10% deposit on the signing of the agreement, a 30% or 35% payment on completion of the hull, a 40% payment on completion of interior joinery, installation of the engine or stepping of the mast, and a 15%-25% payment on completion of acceptance trials and signing of a satisfaction note by the purchaser.

In the case of a small boatyard undertaking a major project, it may be that a higher deposit and first payment will be requested to provide working capital for the purchase of materials and payment of the work force. There is an obvious risk attached to dealing with a yard on this basis and although some protection is given by Clause 11 of the agreement, it would make sense to take out at least bankers' and accountants' references on a small builder before paying over a significant sum of money to him.

The reader will also note the contents of Clause 4.3 which

provides for damages for late delivery. In most cases the boatyard will proffer for approval and signature a copy of the standard form agreement which omits this provision. If that is the case then the intending buyer should insist that the wording be reinstated; it is available in printed form as a separate endorsement to the main agreement from both the sponsoring bodies (RYA and BMIF).

More detailed legal advice on the ordering and purchasing of a new yacht is provided in RYA Booklet G10/93 "Buying a New Yacht".

SALE OF A STOCK BOAT

There is a standard form of contract for the sale of a stock boat published by the BMIF but drafted without the involvement of the RYA, (although the BMIF Standard Terms and Conditions of Business approved by the RYA are incorporated by reference within the agreement).

The value of such an agreement is that a detailed inventory and schedule is included in the contract. A frequent source of argument between the purchaser and dealer arises when the actual boat's specification and gear is different to the original advertised specification, or when detailed additional work ordered by the owner has not been satisfactorily completed. A properly formulated agreement will get round both these potential difficulties.

Although no specific provision is made in the standard form agreement for the final instalment to be held back pending completion of satisfactory sea trials (as in the case of the agreement for the construction of a new craft) it would be wise for the prospective owner to insist on a percentage (say 5%) being reserved for this purpose.

Whereas the new construction agreement refers to instalment (or part) payments, the payment of a deposit to the builder is more likely in the case of the sale of a stock boat. The distinction between a deposit and a part payment is important when purchasing a completed boat either from a business or a private seller.

DEPOSITS AND PART PAYMENTS

A deposit may be of two types :-

(i) A deposit paid as an earnest of good intention in the course of negotiations (intended to lead to the placing of a contract at their conclusion) which, in the event, may break down.
    In such cases, once the negotiations have been discontinued, the recipient of the deposit must return it in full and cannot make any deductions for expenses.
    Where no invoice has been raised no VAT is payable on the amount of such a deposit.

(ii) A deposit paid on the placing of a firm order or the signing of a contract.

Such a payment is generally assumed to be both on account of the purchase price and a "security for performance" and, subject to the terms of the contract, the recipient of the deposit may keep it as compensation for breach of contract, whatever the reasonfor default may be. This general rule can be overridden but it may be found that the contract contains a clearly spelt out notice as to the forfeiture of deposit, in which case there is no argument. Moreover, the contract may contain provisions entitling the other party to both forfeit the deposit and claim any additional sums representing his loss - so read the small print and take advice where appropriate.

A part payment on the other hand is virtually no more than the first instalment of the purchase price paid under a contract. If the order or the contract is cancelled before any goods are delivered or before any work has been done, and this is permitted by the terms of the contract, the normal rule would be that the part payment should be refunded. However, where work has been done, then the other party is first entitled to deduct the cost of that work and all his ancillary administrative expenses.

In a contract providing for payment by instalments it would be usual for the first instalment to be accompanied by the appropriate VAT and this can be refunded in the same proportion.

BANKRUPTCY OF THE BUILDER

This event is the second of the major potential problems. It is important for a purchaser to realise that until the building hull becomes his property, any money paid over to a builder is at risk, in the sense that should the builder become formally insolvent (i.e. a receiver or liquidator appointed) most, if not all of that money will be lost. In such an event the purchaser's status will be only that of an unsecured creditor. Regrettably, numbers of purchasers have over the years found themselves in this position after an apparently well managed and profitable boat building company fails without warning. It is worth bearing this in mind when asked for a large initial deposit and no clear indication of when the first of your money will be spent on the purchase of materials, machinery or fittings for your boat.

In the Contract at Appendix 1, some protection is given to the purchaser by Clause II, but in the case of the purchase of a production/completed boat it is essential to identify the particular boat once it is under construction and early efforts should be made to do this. Once the items which have been paid for are identified or in any way earmarked or attributed to the contract, the liquidator of the company is not entitled to possession of them. Nevertheless, if the contractor/builder has been paid money for the purchase of an engine to put into a craft under construction and he goes into liquidation before the engine is on his premises (or indeed, before he has paid for the engine) the buyer may lose the entire sum.

It is not usually possible for the purchaser to arrange to purchase the engine himself (which would be a safe way to handle the matter). Perhaps the best he can do is to decline to pay for the engine until it is confirmed that the order has been placed by the boat builder. Even then, the money (and property) is not really safe until the engine is delivered and can be adequately identified as appropriated to the contract.

The purchaser should also satisfy himself that those selling a boat are likely to remain solvent and, if they will divulge the information, whether they maintain a separate and properly designated "Client's Account" such as solicitors and other professional persons do.

There have, in the past, been efforts by the RYA and the BMIF to establish a "guarantee" or "bonding" scheme to protect purchasers against default by builders. Unfortunately the potential cost of funding such a scheme proved to be beyond any reasonable sum, and accordingly there is still no formal protection available to purchasers.

The purchase of a ready-made boat presents fewer problems, but it is essential that the purchaser makes certain that any necessary insurance of property in which he has an interest is effected.

ACCEPTANCE TRIALS

Once again, the terms of a contract may be specific about such trials, but in general the purchaser should have a reasonable opportunity of undertaking acceptance trials, the duration of which will obviously vary between craft.

If the purchaser finds fault with the vessel during the acceptance trials then the contract usually requires the vendor to correct them before any final payments are made. Even after acceptance trials have been satisfactorily completed, the acceptance note signed and final money payment made, the purchaser is not debarred from making use of the rules relating to merchantable quality, fitness for the purpose and compliance with description. He has these rights under statute law, and can make use of them.

REPAIR AND CONVERSION

Although the BMIF does not publish a standard form agreement under this heading, their standard schedule of "Estimate of Cost" might be invaluable in the case of a dispute which involves detailed questions of fact as to faults or cost of the work. This schedule itemises labour and materials, overheads and profit percentage into more than one hundred "cost areas". The main headings are shown in Appendix 2.

One of the more frequent causes of complaint by yacht owners against yards is that the cost of work has gone far beyond the agreed quotation or indicated estimate; such complaints could so often be avoided by the parties getting together to agree a written specification and detailed costs at an early stage in their dealings. The section in Chapter 4 dealing with rights under the Supply of Goods & Services Act deals in more detail with this topic.

SELLING THROUGH A BROKER

Unless an owner intends to sell his yacht privately, it makes sense to deal through a member of the YBDSA and ABYA, two organisations which do their best to admit to their ranks only reputable brokers who are prepared to follow the "British Boating Industry Code of Practice".

This agreement provides for a formal "Listing Agreement" (either on sole or joint brokerage) and for the broker to be responsible for obtaining a properly executed Bill of Sale from the seller, for keeping proceeds in a separate account, and for the transfer of funds to the vendor within 14 days of sale or upon transfer of clear title.

Regrettably there are "cowboys" in all walks of life, and the brokerage business is no exception. An occasional ploy (which would not be possible in the case of a broker abiding by the Industry Code of Practice) is the practice of withholding purchase money. This is "justified" by the claim in the case of unregistered yachts that the "transfer of clear title" provision in the contract entitles the broker to withhold the proceeds unless and until the vendor produces documentary proof that he is entitled to sell. This spurious argument is, unfortunately, plausible enough to prevent a civil court giving judgment without a trial, and the unfortunate vendor will have to go through the whole gamut of proceedings to recover his proceeds, while the broker gains the interest on the money. Selling through an ABYA/YBDSA broker, or one found through personal recommendation, is one way to avoid this and similar problems.

The Listing Agreement referred to above should provide that the broker will be entitled to fees and commission only in the event of his introducing a purchaser with whom the transaction proceeds to a successful conclusion. It often happens that a purchaser will see a yacht advertised privately in the classified columns of the yachting press, as well as receiving particulars of the yacht from an agent. In these circumstances it is a simple question of fact as to how the initial introduction was made. If the broker's particulars were issued after the first contact between purchaser and seller, no commission is payable; if the particulars preceded the introduction then a commission is payable.

Where a yacht is berthed in a marina at the time of sale, some berthing agreements still provide for the payment of a fee of 1% (or 2% in some cases) to the marina operator. There is nothing unlawful about removing a yacht from the marina in question during the time of the sale in order to avoid payment of this fee, which in any case is rarely justifiable. If sold privately the fee is paid by the seller, but if through a broker the Code of Practice provides that it should come out of the broker's 8% commission, a provision that is occasionally overlooked by brokers.

CHAPTER 3

YACHT INSURANCE

INSURABLE INTEREST AND VALUE OF THE VESSEL

For a valid contract of insurance to exist, it is necessary for the insured to have an insurable interest; in other words he should either be the owner, charterer, mortgagee of the vessel or have some other beneficial interest.

The Marine Insurance Act 1906 defines an insurable interest as follows:-

(1) Subject to the provisions of this Act, every person has an insurable interest who is interested in a marine adventure.

(2) In particular a person is interested in a marine adventure where he stands in any legal or equitable relation to the adventure or to any insurable property at risk therein, in consequence of which he may benefit by the safety or due arrival of insurable property, or may be prejudiced by its loss, or by damage thereto, or by the detention thereof, or may incur liability in respect thereof.

Section 7 of the Act provides that a contingent interest may be insurable. For example a purchase agreement may provide that the yacht is at the seller's risk until she has arrived at a port nominated by the buyer. In these circumstances the buyer will have no insurable interest in the yacht during the voyage but does have an insurable contingent interest in the arrival. In the case of *Piper -v- Royal Exchange Assurance (1932) 44 LL 103,* Piper bought a yacht in Norway "as she lies". She was at the risk of the seller until she arrived in London. Piper effected a policy in respect of her and claimed against the insurers in respect of damage which she had suffered by going aground on the voyage to London. The insurers paid the claim but were held to be entitled to recover the payment as the risk in the delivery voyage was on the seller, not the buyer.

In addition to establishing an interest, the insured must be careful as to the value he puts on the vessel. The contract of insurance demands total disclosure by the insured of all relevant facts (and that may well extend to facts that may not appear to the insured to be obviously relevant). This applies as much to the value of the yacht as to the other factors affecting the premium. Although it is rarely necessary to obtain a professional valuation, the insured should be careful neither to under-insure nor over-insure the yacht. Over-insurance (i.e. a proposed valuation over market value) will not invalidate the policy unless the underwriter can show that the valuation was so far in excess of the market value as to amount to a material misrepresentation. While it is true that the agreement between insured and underwriter is not for "market value" but rather for "agreed value", too wide a differential between the market value and stated value may give the underwriter grounds for avoiding liability in the event of a claim.

In the case of *Slattery -v- Mance (1962) 1QB 676* a yacht insured for £4,500 at Lloyds suffered a total loss by fire when moored on the River Seine. The yacht had in fact been offered for sale some days before completion of the proposal form at a price of £2,850. The Court held that this differential, going so far beyond the true commercial value of the yacht, amounted to an untrue and material misrepresentation and the underwriters were entitled to repudiate the claim, and the assured did not receive even the market value of £2,850.

When assessing the required value of personal effects to be carried aboard, it should be made clear to the insurers that the total payout in the event of the vessel becoming a total loss should include the full value of personal effects. Unless this is stipulated clearly at the time of the contract, the insurers will only pay up to the full value of the hull and gear as insured, and the owner may be compensated for only a small part of the personal effects he has lost.

THE PROPOSAL FORM

When completing the proposal form therefore the owner must remember that any misrepresentation, or inadequate or false information, may entitle the insurers to deny all liability under the policy.

It is therefore vital to make a full declaration and to consider all aspects when completing the proposal form, even though it may fail to spell out exactly what information is sought by the underwriter.

Since the proposal form does not constitute a contractual offer, the proposer is in no way bound by completing a form. Indeed a new owner would be wise to shop around the insurance market looking for the best quotation. You should remember however that, in insurance as elsewhere, you get what you pay for. While one broker or company may seem to be able to offer very much more attractive terms than another, it pays to examine the actual scope of cover very carefully, (this may vary considerably between companies), and also to find out what you can about the track record of the company when it comes to prompt and full payment of claims.

Completion of the form will involve full particulars of the yacht, her engines, designed speed, cruising waters to be covered, when and where she will be laid up and how. The underwriters will also require particulars of the fire extinguishers provided, the value of the tender and life-raft, and of any other special equipment covered. A cautious underwriter (and they do vary in this respect) will also ask for particulars of the owner and his experience and qualifications, whether he will permit others to use the yacht, and his previous insurance history.

PERIOD OF VALIDITY

In time past, yachts were generally kept in commission for between five and eight months in each year. The modern practice is to extend this period. Many of the headings in an insurance policy do, in fact, provide cover for the whole twelve month period, but you should stipulate the period in commission and the period laid up. If you later decide to extend the period in commission, you should immediately inform your brokers and an additional premium will be negotiated.

THE "STANDARD" POLICY

Insurance at Lloyds will be according to the Institute Yacht Clauses which were originally based on the time-honoured Ship and Goods Policy. To the layman even the improved recent wording is barely comprehensible, particularly when he learns that the whole is to be interpreted in conjunction with the 1906 Marine Insurance Act and a substantial body of decided cases interpreting both the policy and the Act.

It is well worth remembering however that yacht insurance policies are based very much on the tried and tested ship insurance policies which go back over two centuries and although the terms may by quite bewildering to the uninitiated, each paragraph, sentence and phrase has been analysed and interpreted in Court and thus has a definite and agreed meaning.

The fundamental premise running through the insurance policy is that a claim is only payable if there is an element of "fortuity" in the incident giving rise to the claim. Thus, if a lightly rigged yacht is taken to sea in manifestly unsuitable conditions, the loss for instance of the mast may well not be covered since the insurers may claim that the loss was inevitable.

This same principle has been held to apply in the case of yachts with old (and externally apparently sound) wooden masts suffering glued joint failure in relatively mild conditions. For a claim to be paid, the insured must be able to point to an external accidental cause resulting in damage, be it a freak wave, an unusually and unexpectedly strong squall, flotsam in the water, or some breakage on the yacht causing subsequent further damage. If all the insured can do is to show a sunken hull or a lost rig with no evidence that it was the result of a fortuity, then the underwriter will normally not be obliged to pay.

One particular area of difficulty is where a yacht has sunk because a hose has perished, or a skin fitting has been left open and unconnected after the yacht has been relaunched. Here again the underwriter will normally reject a claim on the grounds that the incident was not brought about by an external accident cause.

In such circumstances the broker through whom the individual will normally be dealing will invariably support the stance taken by the underwriter that the policy is not a "maintenance contract" and that the loss is the direct result of the owner failing to renew fittings or rigging on his yacht as it deteriorates with age.

The underwriter is however limited in his reliance on broken equipment or rigging or even inadequate construction as a reason for repudiation of a claim by the 1985 case of "Miss JayJay". The owner of a motor cruiser, which was lightly (perhaps inadequately) built was on passage from Deauville to Hamble in a brisk headwind. She encountered confused and difficult seas even though the weather conditions were by no means extreme. The bow section of the yacht was extensively damaged by the continuous pounding over a period of some hours (although the damage was not discovered until the yacht arrived at Hamble). The underwriters attempted to avoid the claim on the grounds that the damage was caused by inadequate construction rather than by a peril of the sea. In rejecting this argument the Judge said that while inadequate construction was not in doubt, the fact that adverse weather was one of the causes of the damage was sufficient to make this a valid claim under the policy.

THE TERMS OF THE POLICY

Broadly speaking the standard policy will contain four main sections, all of which presuppose the yacht is being used for private pleasure purposes only. The cover includes:-

1. Loss of, or damage by marine perils to, the craft insured, up to the value insured. The cover includes amongst other things sinking, stranding, fire, collision, theft of the vessel, and, following forcible entry, theft of the normal "yacht" contents and fittings.

   Personal effects are not usually included unless specifically agreed. These are more than likely covered by your Householder's Policy.
2. Collision with other craft resulting in damage for which the insured owner may be legally liable. This includes damage to piers, wharves and jetties, etc. Removal of wreck also comes within this section.
3. Any legal liability for injury or loss sustained by "guests" and

"persons" aboard, but excluding paid crew who should be insured separately under an Employers' Liability Policy.
The owner of a yacht should perhaps make it clear to members of his crew that the yacht's policy will not cover their personal gear and that their own household policy will not cover them for accidental loss or damage to their own personal gear unless this has been specifically insured by them.

4. Salvage charges claimed by salvors. Reasonable charges for preventing losses are likely to be paid under most policies, but this is a doubtful area and you should make your contract with the insurance company bearing this in mind.
It is usual for craft having a designed speed of 17 knots or more to be subject to higher premiums (and special conditions) for obvious reasons.

Some companies impose particularly stringent conditions of use, mooring and storage on small fast craft, and the terms offered by different companies should be carefully compared.

TERRITORIAL LIMITS OF INSURANCE

There are three main ranges or areas which, in descending order of cost to the owner, are as follows:-

(a) Full coastal and sea-going cruising within the home trade limits which cover all United Kingdom waters and Continental coasts from Brest to Elbe. Some policies may include Continental inland waters as far south as Paris.
(b) Coastal cruising within ten miles of home port or permanent moorings.
(c) Non-tidal waters of the United Kingdom.

Single voyages and special cruises are rated separately. Owners should therefore consider their programmes carefully. All insurance policies cover the craft whilst it is stored on land inside the United Kingdom.

It goes without saying that any unusual risks which you are intending to incur should be properly insured and declared to the insurers. You should particularly note that cruising through the inland waterways of Europe is not automatically covered in most policies, and therefore needs special mention on your proposal form or before you undertake such a cruise. You will not necessarily be charged an additional premium but must declare your intentions.

ITEMS COVERED IN THE STANDARD POLICY

It is the differing coverage within different policies which causes the majority of the problems for yachtsmen who have to make a claim.

The Lloyds Institute Yacht Clauses specifically cover:-

1. The hull, rigging, sails, motor, tender and "other equipment" which includes a specified list which, in the case of cruising craft, includes one each of most of the obvious necessities which will be those items of equipment that would normally form part of the inventory of a yacht upon sale.
2. Trestles and tarpaulins, but not trailers, although these can be added to the cover by payment of an additional premium.

THE PERILS OF THE SEA

The standard marine insurance policy refers to "perils of the seas" which is thought by many to be a term so vague as to be capable of almost any construction by a marine underwriter. The expression has however been judicially defined as "every accidental circumstance not the result of ordinary wear and tear, delay, or act of the assured, happening in the course of navigation and causing loss to the subject matter of the insurance".

If, for example, a skin fitting has corroded and leaked, and the yacht has consequently sunk, this is not normally a loss that would be recoverable, any more than a motor insurer would pay for the direct consequences of rust damage to a car. Claims have been rejected where rusty rigging (even where the defect is concealed with a mechanical splice or swage) or perished glued joints have resulted in the loss of a mast, or where a fibreglass hull has simply collapsed due to inherent weakness, osmosis or decay at a stress point.

Even so, a rejection of a claim by an underwriter on the ground that the part that failed was worn, weak, or previously damaged, should be critically and logically examined. To carry this argument to an absurd conclusion, no damage would ever be sustained by a yacht that was adequately built; accordingly the underwriter is required to (and usually does) apply the principle of fortuity realistically, having regard to the design of the yacht in question, and the age, size and strength of her spars and fittings.

When damage occurs, or liability for salvage or to a third party is likely to arise, it is important to inform the insurers as soon as possible after the incident, even if it is not at the time envisaged that a claim need be made on the policy. In most cases this will mean informing the broker who will immediately notify the underwriter, and send the assured a claim form.

In all cases the assured must remember that it is up to him to show that the damage or loss has arisen as the result of an insured risk, or at least that an insured risk was, on the balance of probabilities, the cause of the damage.

A claim will not be paid merely because damage has been sustained by a yacht, but only where the owner can show how the damage occurred. In the case of an incident that was witnessed, this will be simple enough, but since many yachts are left to lie on moorings, unattended often for weeks on end, it will often be a matter of detective work, or even conjecture, as to how the damage was sustained. The unexplained crack or hole in the side of the yacht is not likely to cause difficulty; such damage can only have been caused by an insured peril; what is not so easy is the case where a yacht has sunk at her moorings without any obvious clue as to the cause.

Where the damage has left the yacht vulnerable to further damage or decay, the fact that the owner has notified the insurers does not of course exonerate him from taking immediate steps to prevent more damage arising, whether by having the yacht slipped or an area of damage protected from further damage by the elements. The rule in all such cases is that the owner must act as if uninsured and any further loss that can be attributed to his failure to do so will not be payable.

RISKS OF LAUNCHING

This also is valid throughout the year and underwriters will compensate for damage to the craft which results from launching, dry docking, moving, rigging, and unrigging or from an external incident whilst the craft (whether on or off its trailer and detached from the towing vehicle) is on dry land.

FIRE RISKS

This is also valid throughout the year and covers against fire, explosion, lightning strike, aircraft or objects falling from an aircraft. Losses caused by action taken in anticipation or prevention of a fire have been accepted as a proper claim under the insurance policy.

THEFT AND WILFUL DAMAGE

This also is normally valid throughout the year and the underwriters will compensate for damage caused by unlawful theft of the craft and wilful damage caused by a person who is not a member of the policy holder's family. If the theft or damage occurs in a place other than that within the area of a recognised club, the insurance will only cover (except for theft of the entire craft) equipment belonging to the craft which is locked up, locked to the craft or otherwise fixed to the craft. Outboard motors must be attached by means of a lock.

The words "forcible entry" are often important. Simple "theft" of gear, equipment or property insured under this policy is not covered. Payment of a claim on most marine policies is only made "following forcible entry" and even then only on gear, equipment or property specifically insured under the policy.

In the case of motor boats with outdrives, these again will not be insured unless secured to the craft by some form of anti-theft device. It will not be sufficient in the case of their theft to claim that the unbolting of the units amounts to "forcible entry"; the underwriters will not be obliged to pay unless it can be shown that some form of lock was in use.

PREVENTATIVE MEASURES

Insurers will stipulate routine precautions that must be taken by the insured to protect the craft. For example, when the craft is lying idle it shall be kept free from water and must be adequately moored, anchored and supervised.

EXCEPTIONS

There is a considerable list of exceptions where underwriters will not compensate. These are, briefly, as follows:-

- Where safety precautions have not been observed.
- Where the craft is being used to earn money.
- If damage is caused deliberately, or through gross negligence amounting to wilfulness.
- If the craft is not properly equipped.
- The loss of an outboard motor dropped overboard.
- Damage caused by, or consisting of, faulty construction or materials, lack of seaworthiness, neglect or contamination.
- No payment will be made for loss of time or other indirect loss or for damage to buoys, moorings, etc., which should be separately insured.

SAILS

The standard Lloyds policy provides a specific exclusion for sails and sail covers "split by the wind or blown away while set". This ambiguously worded phrase has been interpreted by the Courts to allow the underwriter to reject any claim for sail damage, whether stowed or set, unless in consequence of damage to a spar.

In the case of a stowed roller-furling genoa, or a mainsail tied to the boom, damage to those is excluded by the first part of the exception "sails split by the wind". The Courts have held that the words "while set" apply only to "sails blown away", it not being necessary for a sail to be set for the underwriter to avoid liability for sails split by the wind. Thus the careful yachtsman will always unrig his roller furling genoa and mainsail before leaving the yacht whether for the laying-up season or just for a week in mid-season.

LACK OF DUE DILIGENCE

Whilst discussing exceptions for which underwriters will not normally compensate, it is worthwhile reiterating that the insured has a general duty of care which is somewhat indefinable and is referred to in most policies by the phrase "due diligence". It is quite reasonable for an insurance company to anticipate that the insured person will be as diligent as possible in protecting and managing his property. It is not, as a lot of people think, sufficient to say:- "oh! leave it there, it's insured", or to take another example, to allow a vessel to drift on to a lee shore, merely because you have been so "lacking in due diligence" as not to provide it with proper anchors.

Section 55 Marine Insurance Act 1906 provides however that the insurer is liable for any loss proximately caused by a peril insured against. S.55 (2) provides that he is not liable for any loss attributable to the wilful misconduct of the assured, but unless the policy otherwise provides, he is liable for any loss proximately caused by a peril insured against, even though the loss would not have happened but for the misconduct of the master or crew.

In the case of negligent or unskilful navigation, the Courts will normally hold that the loss is caused proximately by perils of the seas, and only remotely by the negligence or unskillfulness of the master or crew.

EXCESS

As with any insurance, if an owner is prepared to bear the first loss of, say, £200, his premium may be materially reduced.

RACING RISKS

Considerable additional risks are likely to be incurred whilst racing and different policies have varying requirements as to the loss of, for example, spars, rigging or sails. What is certain is that an extra premium must, quite reasonably, be paid.

A misconception that frequently arises is that retirement or acceptance of an alternative penalty following an infringement whilst racing can prejudice a civil claim for negligence, or amount to the sort of admission of liability that entitles insurers to repudiate a claim. It is important to remember that an act or error of judgment that may be an infringement of the racing rules will only sometimes amount to negligence for the purposes of the civil law. The RYA Prescription to IYR Rule 76.1 specifically provides that the findings of fact of a protest committee can only be brought into evidence in a civil court with the written consent of both parties; in other words such findings are irrelevant to the question of liability for damage.

It would also be quite wrong for an insurer to avoid a claim simply because an owner has acknowledged an infringement of the racing rules in retiring from a race after a collision. Rule 33.1 requires a yacht which realises she has infringed a rule to retire or take a penalty. If a yacht is covered for racing risks then that cover implies an acceptance by the underwriter of the precise terms of the IYR

Rules and RYA prescriptions. Thus the duty to retire is not in conflict with the requirement of certain underwriters that no action should be taken which may be construed as an admission of liability.

VALUE INSURED

If household goods are insured for less than their real value some insurers will apply "average" to any claim (however small) and settle the claim in the same proportion as the under-insurance. Although in a marine policy the concept of average does not apply in the same way, it is important from year to year to settle the exact value of what you own and to agree a realistic value with the insurance company.

CHARTERING

As will be seen from the list of exceptions, when a vessel is being used to earn money underwriters will not compensate unless they have been previously notified. This point should be carefully noted by those who have decided to charter their own vessel in order to defray some of the running costs. If it is intended to charter, this fact must be reported to your brokers so that they may obtain cover; underwriters will normally demand an additional premium.

THIRD PARTY INSURANCE AND MARINE LIMITATION

The standard yacht policy provides an indemnity for property damage or personal injury caused to third parties. Most insurance companies will allow a figure of £1,000,000 although some will only allow £500,000. In either event it should be understood that these high figures will rarely be approached, even if a particularly bad accident is caused by the insured, as the Merchant Shipping Act Limitation of Liability provisions will normally apply. These provisions are not usually referred to in a yacht policy but they do over-ride anything which may be in the policy.

Although the limitation figures have been substantially increased, yacht owners and insurers may still limit liability, even in respect of the negligent handling of a yacht. The Merchant Shipping Act 1979 which came into force on 1st December 1986 allows owners and insurers to limit liability in the case of property damage to 83,333 International Units of Account and to 166,667 IUA in the case of loss of life or personal injury. At 1993 values, these figures give sterling equivalents of approximately £66,000 and £132,000 respectively. See Chapter 5 for fuller details of limitation principles in negligence claims.

CLAIMS

It is when a claim arises that the need for meticulous accuracy in completing the proposal form, and attention to detail in reading the small print in your insurance policy, becomes apparent. Even where the owner has been careful to provide the underwriter with all the information he might require, or be thought to require, and has studied his policy in detail, there are a number of basic concepts governing marine insurance which are not obvious to the layman simply reading the "Yacht Clauses" provided with his certificate of insurance.

The fundamental point to bear in mind is that the insurance contract is not a maintenance contract; it is intended to provide protection against accidents caused by some fortuitous circumstance rather than an inevitability.

In all cases the assured must remember that it is up to him to show that the damage or loss has arisen as the result of an insured risk, or at least that an insured risk was, on the balance of probabilities, the cause of the damage.

When damage occurs, or liability for salvage or to a third party is likely to arise, it is important to inform the insurers as soon as possible after the incident, even if it is not at the time envisaged that a claim need be made on the policy. In most cases this will mean informing the broker who will immediately notify the underwriter, and send the assured a claim form.

APPOINTMENT OF SURVEYORS

Once a claim has been made, if physical damage has been done to the yacht, the underwriter will usually appoint a surveyor to inspect the damage and make recommendations for repairs. Although it is not unusual for a surveyor to try to do so, he is not authorised to give repair instructions to the boatyard; the yard is employed by the yacht owner and it is from the owner that any directions must come. The function of the surveyor is merely to advise the underwriter in his dealings with the owner. If the surveyor approves the claim and agrees the estimate for repairs, it is for the broker, acting on the underwriter's instructions, to inform the owner, and for the owner to give the go-ahead to the yard to carry out repairs. In all cases the owner should ensure that a fully agreed schedule of works is prepared in advance and agreed with the yard. This list should be enclosed with the instruction that additional items of work found to be necessary should not be dealt with until approved by the underwriter's surveyors, or specifically authorised by the owner.

Most underwriters will, as a matter of policy, not disclose the contents of a surveyor's report to the assured, who may only guess at the contents of the report by the underwriter's attitude to the claim.

Since it is the function of the underwriter's surveyors to ensure that his principal is exposed to the minimum proper cost for the job, it is inevitable that conflicts of opinion as to what constitutes adequate repair will arise. In such cases, especially if there is a material difference of opinion, the owner may wish to appoint his own surveyor to report on the damage and recommend repairs. Where this is done a compromise settlement will usually be possible, but if the dispute remains unresolved then his own surveyor's report will form the basis of his case if the dispute has to go to court.

BROKER ACTS FOR THE ASSURED

Throughout the conduct of a claim, all communications between the assured and the underwriter will be channelled through the broker (unless the assured is dealing with the claims department of a company). It is important to remember that the broker acts for the assured, and while he cannot of course fabricate evidence, or encourage the assured to do so, he should be prepared to be tough with the underwriter where necessary, not just act as a post box.

Although most insurance claims will be negotiated and settled without a hitch, it occasionally arises that the assured, despite representations made on his behalf by the broker, is dissatisfied with the underwriter's final decision.

In the case where a yacht is insured at Lloyds, the assured may call for the question to be referred to the Consumer Enquiries Department at Lloyds, which will then initiate its own in-house investigation into the underwriter's repudiation of the claim in part or in whole. In the event of the underwriter's action being supported by the internal inquiry, and the assured still being dissatisfied, then beyond further negotiation the only course of action is to take the matter to court. In this case the assured will be well advised to go to a solicitor experienced in the specialised field of marine insurance.

A claim will occasionally be repudiated on the grounds that the owner was not insured at all. This will most frequently arise as a result of a misunderstanding between the owner and broker as to the exact dates of cover, exclusions, or cruising range, and illustrates the necessity of meticulous care in all dealings with the insurance market.

If an owner is able to show that the failure arises from an incompetent or careless act of the broker, then the general principles of negligence may be relied upon and action taken accordingly. While the need for such action is rare, such circumstances do arise and indeed all insurance brokers carry professional indemnity insurance to cover such an eventuality.

PAYMENT OF THE CLAIM

A concept that is often difficult to understand for the layman who is perhaps more familiar with motor or household insurance, is that his policy is a contract of indemnity on which no payment need be made until the full measure of damage is known, and repairs and renewals have been carried out and paid for.

In the case of damage to a motor car, or to a household appliance, the underwriter will normally take direct responsibility for payment to the repairer; in contrast with this the yacht underwriter will only make a single final payment when presented with all the receipted bills together with a satisfaction note signed by the assured.

It is important, therefore, to distinguish the separate stages in an insurance claim:

- notification to insurer
- survey by insurer
- negotiation if necessary leading to an agreement on what work will be paid for by insurer
- authorisation of work by insured and payment of yard bill by him
- reimbursement by insurer on production of the receipted bill.

CHAPTER 4

CONSUMER PROTECTION

INTRODUCTION

Any private owner of a yacht or small craft who enters into transactions with suppliers, repairers, riggers, sailmakers, insurers, surveyors, or any one of the many trades or professions associated with the sport of yachting should be constantly aware of his rights not only under the common law but also under the various Acts of Parliament which together provide this country's Consumer Protection legislation.

It is an unfortunate fact of life that many perfectly businesslike people who would not consider accepting anything less than the best in, for example, the construction or repair of a house, a household appliance or a new car, will frequently be prepared to accept second-rate service when it comes to dealing with the yachting trade.

Although there are organisations like the British Marine Industries Federation (and its affiliated organisations) which properly expect a sound track record from potential members before accepting them into membership, the yacht owner should be constantly on the lookout for the less scrupulous operators who abound in this market.

It is important that the owner should be totally familiar with the protection that the law now affords him and, equally, aware of the importance of dealing only with reputable firms under the terms of a fair contract.

THE CONTRACT

Whatever your dealings with the yachting trade, it is likely that major transactions will be covered by one of the many standard forms of contract available either through the trade or the RYA. Any private individual dealing with a BMIF member, or a member of an affiliated (or affinitive) organisation such as the Yacht Brokers, Designers and Surveyors Association, or the Association of Brokers and Yacht Agents, can and should insist on doing business along the lines of one of the standard form contracts. Before entering into any agreement, it is well worth taking a long unhurried look at the relevant contract, and ensuring that you fully understand the implications of all the clauses, and of any clause or option that may be added or omitted by agreement.

REPAIR AND CONVERSION

Although the BMIF does not publish a standard form agreement under this heading, their schedule of "Estimate of Cost" (in which agreed construction or conversion work on a yacht can be analysed, as to labour and materials, overheads and profit percentage, into over one hundred different cost areas) would be invaluable in the case of dispute which involved detailed questions of fact as to faults or cost of the work.

One of the more frequent causes of complaint by yacht owners against yards is that the cost of work has gone far beyond the agreed or indicated estimate; such complaints could so easily be avoided by the parties getting together to agree a specification and detailed costs at an early stage. Too often an owner tells the contractor to get on with repairs, and to do anything else he comes across that needs attention. In those circumstances the yard can hardly be blamed for running up bills greatly in excess of the original proposal.

In the event that a boatyard refuses to give a firm quotation, on the grounds that the extent of the work required to be done will not be evident until some dismantling or remedial work has already taken place, written instructions should be given that no further work be carried out without written authority, or an agreed price ceiling applied. Much of this is common sense but it is too easy to allow the cost of conversion or repair to run away unless tight control is maintained.

STATUTORY CONSUMER PROTECTION

Apart from the terms of any contract, which governs the basic relationship between the consumer and supplier, Parliament has enacted a number of measures to make the position of the consumer even more secure.

Sale of Goods Act 1979

The most frequently invoked protection is that provided by the Sale of Goods Act 1979 which protects every person who enters into a contract to buy (or hire) goods, as a consumer. Although the Act runs to sixty-four sections the consumer will be most frequently concerned with Section 12 (Legal Right of the Seller to Sell the Goods) Section 13 (Goods to correspond with the Seller's description or sample) and Section 14 (Goods to be fit for the purpose for which they are required and of merchantable quality).

Section 12 imposes a condition that the buyer has a right to sell the goods. If he is not the owner, or a third party has an interest in the goods, the condition imposed by the Act will operate to protect the buyer whether or not the seller knew of his defective title (unless there is an agreement with the buyer to the contrary).

Where there is a breach of the implied condition in Section 12, the buyer will have the right to repudiate the contract and claim his money back, as well as damages for any resulting loss. An undisclosed mortgage or lien on a yacht would be a breach of this condition. This section frequently comes into operation where goods have been stolen and subsequently change hands honestly. In such cases the thief will have made off with the proceeds, leaving the original owner and one or two subsequent buyers to pick up the pieces. In those circumstances the true owner will be able to claim back the goods, and the second buyer will be entitled to the return of the purchase price. The first buyer who purchased the goods from the thief will just have to write it off to experience. To be able to enforce such a right, the eventual purchaser must be able to trace and claim or proceed against the intermediate purchaser; if this person has disappeared or is unreachable, the loss in practice will lie with the eventual purchaser. This should be borne in mind, e.g. when buying a boat without any proof of title.

Section 13 imposes a condition that, where goods are sold by description, any part of that description amounting to a material misdescription will give a right to repudiate the contract, or at least to claim damages. This section would be relevant to the purchaser of a vessel where the agreed specification was changed. Even if the craft is capable of modification so as to comply, unless the difference in specification is minimal, the consumer is entitled to repudiate the agreement.

The old Common Law rule of "Caveat Emptor" (let the buyer beware) is repeated in **Section 14** subject to provisions which impose a general condition that the goods must be of merchantable quality, and a specific condition that they must be fit for their purpose.

It is important to remember that the protection which this section gives to a purchaser only applies to goods sold in the course of business.

The section goes on to define merchantable quality as being as fit "for the purpose...... for which goods of that kind are commonly bought as it is reasonable to expect having regard to any description applied to them, the price (if relevant) and all the other relevant circumstances".

It is suggested that minor defects of appearance, minor missing items etc. are no longer relevant to the concept of "merchantable quality" though they may be relevant in the context of "fitness for purpose". For example the buyer of a new boat rightly expects to receive something that is not seriously scratched or shoddily finished.

Section 14 also provides that, where goods are sold in the course of a business and the buyer makes known to the seller, expressly or impliedly, the purpose for which the goods are required, there is an implied condition that the goods will be reasonably fit for that purpose. The provision does not apply where the buyer evidently did not, or could not have, relied upon the seller's "skill and judgment". The seller is not held to promise that the goods are absolutely suitable; a boat or piece of equipment may be reasonably fit for its purpose even though it is known to require repairs. On the other hand, even a minor defect making the goods unfit will give the buyer the chance to reject the goods so long as he does so in good time. For example, the main inland navigation authorities have stringent construction and equipment standards. If, to the knowledge of the seller, a boat is bought with those standards in mind and fails to pass the scrutiny of the Authority's inspector, then the buyer is entitled to repudiate the contract unless the defect is really trivial.

In the event that the buyer would rather have the defects put right then he is entitled to claim damages i.e. a money payment sufficient to mend the defect. As a matter of convenience (though not a strict legal right) such work is often done by the seller at no charge.

In dealing with cases under the Sale of Goods Act, there are two important principles to remember....... first: do not delay in pursuing your rights, the trail may go cold, the court may decide that you have "accepted" the goods notwithstanding the defects, or you may be deemed to have had sufficient use of the goods to prejudice your rights to full redress (in particular, delay in rejecting faulty goods immediately the defect is discovered is likely to mean the loss of the right to reject, and you will be left only with a claim for the cost of putting the defect right: this can be highly inconvenient)....... second: always pursue your complaint against the seller, not against the manufacturer or builder (unless they are one and the same person). Do not be put off by the seller referring you back to the manufacturer, the seller is the only one under any direct obligation under the Sale of Goods Act to put matters right.

You need only concern yourself with any additional "guarantee" provided by the manufacturer if the seller of the goods is unable to satisfy his contractual obligations.

Misrepresentation Act 1967

It has always been possible to claim damages from somebody (whether he is in business or not) if you have entered into a contract with him after, and as a result of, a fraudulent misrepresentation. However this Act provides that even an innocent misrepresentation can render the person making the statement liable for damages unless he can show that he had reasonable grounds for believing that whatever he said or wrote was true. Furthermore, any misrepresentation can in certain circumstances entitle the person to whom it was made to rescind the resulting contract. In addition, any attempt (usually by a term in a standard form printed contract) to exclude potential liability under this Act will succeed only to the extent that the exclusion is, in the circumstances, reasonable.

A selling agent must be careful not to pass on more information about, for example, a yacht than that given to him by the owner. Otherwise, if that information is erroneous, he might be liable not only to the owner, but also to the buyer.

Any person making statements about goods in anticipation of selling them must ensure that such statements are not only accurate, but in no way misleading. For example, to tell a prospective buyer that a yacht had been involved in a collision without also telling him that she sank as a result might render the seller liable to damages for misrepresentation.

Especially with second hand boats there is considerable scope for misunderstandings and in general the buyer is legally in a strong position if he is misled. He may know he was misled; but argument and negotiation may fail and to prove his case he may be faced with the prospect of expensive and protracted litigation, with all its risks. Better by far to be circumspect about relying on any statements; the wise buyer will obtain a proper survey of the boat, will insist on a proper sea trial, and will discover any defects before parting with the balance of the agreed price.

Trade Description Act 1968

This is an Act with a "criminal" application and is not, therefore, of much use to an innocent buyer pursuing a civil claim against a seller. Broadly, it makes the giving of a false or misleading trade description, in relation to goods, a criminal offence which could result, on summary conviction, in a fine of up to £400 and, on conviction on indictment, to up to two years' imprisonment.

Any person in the course of a trade or business could be liable. His defence could be that somebody else made the mistake, he committed the offence by mistake, or that he took all reasonable precautions and exercised due diligence to avoid making a false trade description.

The words "trade description" are very broad and include such matters as methods of manufacture; fitness for purpose, strength, performance; behaviour or accuracy. So if a chandler is asked "will this rope withstand a load of 4,000 lbs?" he must not reply carelessly or he may be liable under this Act, although his liability will be criminal and will not give the buyer any direct rights. The buyer will, of course, have rights against him under the Sale of Goods Act or The Misrepresentation Act.

The Act also applies to the trade publisher of advertisements unless he can show that he did not know, and had no reason to suspect, that the publication of a particular advertisement would amount to an offence.

It is also an offence for any person in the course of any trade or business to make a statement that he knows to be false; or recklessly to make a statement which is false as to the provision or nature (in the course of any trade or business) of any services, accommodation or facilities, or as to the time at or manner in which these may be available.

Unfair Contract Terms Act 1977

The main provisions of this Act, which extend to the provision of services as well as the supply of goods, apply to those seeking to exclude or restrict liabilities arising in the course of running a business.

The main provisions of the Act may be summarised as follows:-

(i) A person may not, whether by a term in a contract or a public notice, exclude or restrict his liability for any death or personal injury caused by his negligence.

(ii) A person when dealing with a consumer or on standard written terms of business cannot, by reference to a term in the relevant contract, protect himself against a legal claim if he fails to fulfil the main terms of the contract except insofar as it is in the circumstances reasonable for him to do so.

(iii) As against a consumer, any attempt by a supplier (whether of goods or services) to cover himself against liability to third parties for breach of the relevant contract, or negligence by the expedient of obtaining an indemnity from the consumer, will be unenforceable (again except to the extent that it is in the circumstances reasonable for him to do so).

(iv) A "manufacturer's guarantee" in relation to goods usually supplied for private use can no longer operate to restrict the liability of a manufacturer or distributor for a defect in those goods caused by his negligence.

(v) The warranties and conditions implied in a contract for the sale of goods (which were discussed in the section on the Sale of Goods Act) apply equally (to such an extent as may be appropriate) to any contract for the supply of goods (e.g. hire, hire-purchase, exchange, a contract for work and materials etc.).

It will be noted from the above that the concept of "reasonableness" is of importance.

What is "reasonable"? The Act says, "In relation to a contract term the requirement of reasonableness..... is that the term shall have been a fair and reasonable one to be included having regard to the circumstances which were, or ought reasonably to have been, known to or in the contemplation of the parties when the contract was made".

The Act then sets out guidelines for helping to determine what is reasonable, in relation to contracts for the supply of goods. In layman's terms, these are:-

(i) the relative strength of the bargaining positions of both parties;
(ii) whether the consumer was financially induced to accept the term in his contract;
(iii) whether he could have got the same contract without restriction from anybody else;
(iv) whether he knew of the relevant term or might reasonably have been expected to realise that it was in the contract;
(v) whether the goods were manufactured etc. to his special order.

The Act affects the validity of many contract terms and notices currently used in business and, so far as boat owners or users are concerned, serves to protect them further. It should be borne in mind that as a result of the Act, certain contract clauses (even if still included in a standard form contract) many now be unenforceable.

The Supply of Goods and Services Act 1979

Although the terms of the Act did not provide any new safeguards for the consumer, it was introduced to codify the law and in effect made it simpler for the consumer or client to understand his rights.

The effect of the Act is to imply terms (in the same way as the Sale of Goods Act in its own context) about the standard of care and skill to be expected in a contract for services and about the time to be taken for the performance of the contract. It is also laid down that the price (if not agreed in advance) may not be more than is reasonable in the circumstances. This last term will be of particular relevance in those many cases involving failure by a boat yard to comply with an estimate or quotation. The Act will not, of course, provide guidance as to what is fair and reasonable, this being a question of fact, but it will emphasise the right of a consumer, who is misled by a low estimate, to bring a counter-claim for negligence on the part of the estimator even though the consumer might be under an initial contractual liability to pay the amount demanded. The effect of this is that the successful counter-claim may wipe out the excess of the final invoice over the original estimate or quotation.

Consumer Protection Act 1987

This Act was brought into force to comply with the requirements of the European Community "Product Liability Directive" to harmonise European law on liability for defective products.

Any person who produces, imports into the EC area, or holds

himself out as the producer of any product is liable for any damage caused wholly or partly by a defect in the product.

A product is defined as defective if the safety of the product is not such as persons generally are entitled to expect, and damage to property as well as death or personal injury is covered by the Act.

Section 5 (2) of the Act makes it clear that damage to the product itself is not covered. There must be consequential damage to other property (or death or personal injury). Where property is damaged, the Act will only apply where it is property ordinarily intended for private use or occupation or consumption, and intended by the person suffering the loss or damage mainly for his own private use or occupation, and the damage must be in excess of £275 for liability to arise.

In addition to the civil claim, Part II of the Act imposes criminal liability on any person who supplies consumer goods which fail to comply with the general safety requirement.

The Act also provides an extension to the normal time limitation period of six years by allowing a plaintiff to take action any time up to ten years after the cause of action has arisen.

Since the Act has only been in force since March 1988 it is still not clear how effective a remedy is provided by the new legislation. Hitherto an aggrieved purchaser of defective equipment which causes consequential damage to other equipment or death or personal injury could only bring an action against the supplier (not the manufacturer) under the contract, or against the manufacturer if there was evidence of negligence on the part of the manufacturer. The position of the consumer is now much stronger in that the manufacturer is now directly liable to the ultimate consumer without negligence having to be proved against him.

RESOLUTION OF DISPUTES

However prudent an owner may have been in selecting a competent and trustworthy member of the trade, there is always the risk of a dispute arising out of a disagreement over the terms of the contract, the standard of work or the price to be paid. In these circumstances an owner can rapidly find himself running up enormous (and frequently unnecessary) professional fees.

In the event of a dispute or a potential dispute arising, the first step should always be to contact the other party and make a genuine attempt to settle the problem. Unless an owner feels strongly that he is being deliberately "taken for a ride", or the sum at stake is considerable, it always makes sense to try to reach a compromise settlement rather than sue, or defend proceedings.

If dealing with a small limited company, firm or "one-man-band", the plaintiff may well pause to consider whether a firm is worth suing - many small firms lead a precarious financial existence and a High Court judgment with costs may be beyond their resources. Indeed, in the yachting business as elsewhere there are those who go into liquidation when faced with proceedings from disaffected customers only to re-emerge shortly afterwards with the same staff, same premises and same stock but under a different name.

If it becomes clear that there is no prospect of agreement, then swift action must be taken to secure professional advice to establish exactly what rights and liabilities exist, and what procedure should be followed.

The Royal Yachting Association legal department is able to provide "first aid" advice to members in dispute with the trade, and very often can guide members should it prove necessary to instruct solicitors to handle their case. While many members will have their own retained "family solicitors", shipping litigation is a specialised field of law and many family solicitors will be the first to admit to a lack of experience in this area.

In many cases involving disputes of fact (e.g. standard of work/ fairness of price) rather than of law (e.g. exact meaning of the terms of a contract) the owner will be advised to go first to an independent surveyor to obtain a professional opinion on the issue, and the other party to a dispute may often be prevailed upon to cover the cost in part or in whole of a limited survey and report. Such a report may at best provide an immediate solution to a dispute if the contractor is willing to accept the findings and recommendations of the surveyor; it will at least provide useful guidance to the owner and his solicitor as to how the case should be handled if it is then decided to take it to court.

As in the choice of solicitors, it is essential to choose a surveyor with the right qualifications and experience. It should be borne in mind that if a negotiated settlement proves impossible, when the surveyor has to appear in Court as an expert witness, the success of a case may well turn on the impression that he makes on the judge or arbitrator, as much as on the evidence that he actually gives.

Having chosen his legal adviser and surveyor, or having collated all the evidence himself, the owner must then take the decision whether to initiate court proceedings in the County Court or High Court, or to take advantage of the BMIF/RYA arbitration scheme.

County Court

If the sum total of the claim is £50,000 or less, then proceedings may be initiated in the County Court within whose jurisdiction the Defendant resides or carries on business or where the original contract was agreed or cause of action arose. Since County Court proceedings are generally cheaper, simpler and speedier than

High Court proceedings, it will often be worthwhile cutting down the amount of a claim to a sum "not exceeding £50,000" to stay within the limit of jurisdiction.

Court procedure is not within the scope of this booklet. If a solicitor is employed it may be left safely in his hands. If the owner is acting in person then the County Court staff will always be prepared to help and advise on procedural matters. County Courts operate a "small claims" procedure with a simplified process designed to remove the need for lawyer involvement. This is compulsory for claims less than £500.00 and may be used, if both parties agree, for higher sums. A free booklet describes the process can be obtained from the court. The £500.00 limit may well soon be raised to £1000.00.

High Court

Claims in excess of £50,000 must be issued in the High Court, where one can expect procedures to be more involved, time delays to be greater, and costs higher.

In High Court proceedings, professional advice and representation is almost essential unless the owner is prepared to invest a lot of his own time and energy to act in person.

Private Arbitration

Most standard forms of contract will provide that any dispute arising between the parties will be submitted to an independent arbitrator appointed (failing an agreement between the parties) by the BMIF or RYA. In practice both these bodies appoint arbitrators from a jointly agreed list.

The advantage of a private arbitration is that the arbitrator will normally have general expert knowledge of the problem in question, proceedings are very much faster and less formal and there is rarely any need to employ professional legal advisers, although the arbitrator may well agree to hear evidence from a surveyor if one has been instructed by either of the parties.

The disadvantage of arbitration is that the arbitrator will not have the same legal background as a judge, and will usually tend to look for a compromise solution rather than coming down firmly on one side or another. As a general rule a dispute involving questions of fact alone may safely be left with an arbitrator; questions of law and legal construction are not suitable for a non-legally qualified arbitrator and should be taken to court. A further problem is that rights of appeal from the decision of an arbitrator may be excluded.

DAMAGES

Where the court is asked to award damages in respect of a breach of contract (and a claim can be for damages alone, damages plus rescission of the contract and return of the purchase price, or damages plus some other order of the court) careful thought must be given by the plaintiff to the exact sum sought.

The principle behind an award is that the successful plaintiff should so far as possible be compensated for all losses arising from the defendant's breach of contract. He should, as far as money can do it, be placed in the same position as if the contract had been fully performed. In assessing damages the court will only take account of strict, legal obligations; it cannot take account of the expectations of one party to the contract that the other will do something that he is under no obligation to do. Of course, if the Plaintiff cannot establish actual loss he is only entitled to nominal damages.

The approach of the courts in assessing the total loss resulting from a breach of contract is well illustrated in the recent case of Sutherland -V- Senator Yachts (1988). The Plaintiff bought a Senator 37 trawler yacht in 1981, taking delivery of her in Palma, Mallorca, and intending to use her for skippered charter cruises. Believing the two-year-old ex-demonstrator model to be in good condition, he bought the boat unseen. Having paid £39,000 he found a number of major faults including an unserviceable generator, a faulty engine cooling system and a split masthead. Another problem was the boat's range which was advertised as 830 miles at six knots, but turned out to be just 350 miles. This made the boat unsuitable for the plaintiff's requirements and he asked the Defendant company to take the boat back. Their response was to claim that he still owed them £2500 for maintenance costs; the boat was arrested in Malta, and the Plaintiff and his crew were forced to leave it to go home. The High Court awarded the Plaintiff £115,000, plus costs, when he sued for breach of contract. The award took into account expenses and the loss of charter earnings as well as the original price of the boat which, it was held, the plaintiff was entitled to reject.

CHAPTER 5

LIABILITY TO OTHER WATER USERS

The United Kingdom remains one of the few countries in the developed world where a yachtsman is free to take his craft to sea without either passing a driving test and obtaining a licence for himself, or requiring a licence or registration for his yacht and subjecting it to type approval or other safety inspection procedures.

Throughout the 18th and 19th centuries the development of statute law sponsored by the Board of Trade left pleasure craft largely untouched; at the time yachting was the sport of kings and the nobility, and to encompass their yachts in legislation which was primarily designed to control the use and design of merchant shipping would have been unthinkable.

The exemption for persons navigating pleasure yachts from the requirement to hold certificates of competency is enshrined in Section 262 Merchant Shipping Act 1894.

In modern times the continuing exemption of small private pleasure craft from legislation can be attributed to the awareness and safety conscious attitudes of British yachtsmen who are able to behave responsibly without the necessity for legislation.

Where, however, a yachting accident does occur involving damage, injury or loss of life, the law will normally demand proof of a high standard of seamanship and ship management from a person defending a claim for negligence by an injured party.

PRINCIPLES OF LIABILITY IN COLLISION CASES

The most common cause of liability arising on behalf of the yacht owner will be that of collision. Although all navigators are presumed to have knowledge of the International Regulations for Preventing Collisions at Sea (and the associated rules for lights and sound signals) errors of judgment do occur and, where an injured party is able to show negligence on the part of the defendant, there will be a liability to compensate the plaintiff to the full extent of his loss as described below. Although any legal action will be dealt with by a Court of Admiralty jurisdiction, the principles of liability follow those applying in any action for negligence. The plaintiff must prove that the defendant was in breach of his duty of care, and the Court will hear evidence on all the circumstances of the collision (not just evidence that there was a breach of the IRPCS), and the defendant will be entitled, where appropriate, to raise the defences of contributory negligence, inevitable accident and volenti non fit injuria (i.e. a willing participant in a risky activity cannot generally complain of injury or damage).

Where a collision occurs between racing yachts, a misconception which frequently arises is that retirement or acceptance of an alternative penalty following an infringement can prejudice a civil claim for negligence, or amount to the sort of admission of liability that entitles insurers to repudiate a claim. It is important to remember that an act or error of judgment that may be an infringement of the racing rules will only sometimes amount to negligence for the purposes of the civil law. The RYA prescription to IYR rule 76.1 specifically provides that the findings of fact of a protest committee can only be brought into evidence in a civil court with the written consent of both parties; in other words such findings are irrelevant to the question of liability for damage.

It would also be quite wrong for an insurer to avoid a claim simply because an owner has acknowledged an infringement of the racing rules by retiring from a race after a collision. If a yacht is covered for racing risks then that cover implies an acceptance by the underwriter of the precise terms of the IYR rules and RYA prescriptions. Rule 33.1 requires a yacht which realises she has infringed a rule to retire or take a penalty. Thus the duty to retire prevails over the requirement of certain underwriters that no action should be taken which may be construed as an admission of liability.

There is of course an infinite variety of circumstances in which two or more yachts or ships can come into contact with each other causing anything from a superficial scratch in the gel-coat to a total loss. Weather conditions, visibility, other navigational hazards and mechanical failure, all play a significant part in the circumstances leading to a collision or "near miss", but most importantly the seamanship, foresight and intelligent appraisal of others' moves by the skipper or watch leader are the prerequisites of safety at sea.

When a collision case comes to court for adjudication it will be decided not according to any uniquely legal principles, but in accordance with the facts of the case as they appear in the light of common sense.

Negligence charged in collision cases may not necessarily be negligence in navigation. It can be negligence in the management of the yacht. Failure to care adequately for equipment, a breakdown of steering gear due to neglect or carelessness, or the parting of a mooring rope for the same reasons, could amount to actionable fault. A successful defence to such an allegation would be that the defect was latent, i.e. not discoverable even by the exercise of due diligence, or that the yacht had been taken to sea in as efficient and safe a condition as the exercise of reasonable care could ensure.

MEASURE OF PROPERTY DAMAGE

The successful plaintiff will be entitled to full compensation for all his losses arising from an incident excepting those regarded in law as too remote. If there is a total loss the owner will be compensated to the full market value. Where repairable damage has been caused, the cost of repair is recoverable, together with any towage, salvage, harbour dues, survey fees or delivery costs.

If a yacht is damaged, the owner is under an obligation to make all reasonable efforts to minimise the loss, including preventing her from sinking, and he must not refuse reasonable offers of help, nor must he unreasonably abandon her.

In addition there will be recoverable any expenses suffered by the crew and the cost to the owner of the loss of the use of his yacht (which may even be measured by the cost of chartering an alternative vessel for the time that the owner's damaged craft is out of commission).

When the owner loses the use of his yacht for some time as a result of damage, and a successful claim is made, it is sometimes difficult to assess the damages recoverable for loss of use. This is because the yacht is not employed for profit and there is no obvious financial loss arising from her non-availability. The owner will be entitled to more than merely nominal damages, the loss of pleasure being a ground for an award even though this is not accurately measurable.

Special circumstances such as a clear demand for the charter of the yacht at the time of collision will sometimes provide a basis of assessment. In the case of The Fortunity (1960) a yacht built, owned and maintained solely for letting to the public on the Norfolk Broads had damages assessed in this way, on the basis of the yacht as a business asset, together with a further sum for loss of profit on bookings. In the case of a private pleasure yacht however the court may consider that the proper course is to allow a sum corresponding to the loss of reasonable interest on the capital invested in the yacht during the time the owner is deprived of her use. This approach was taken in the case of The Zoroaster (1903). Another approach is shown by the Irish case of The Anglican (1873) where it was proved that the yacht was lowered in value by the fact of repair damage after collision and, though the owner had no intention of selling her, he was held entitled to compensation under this head.

If of course the owner were to hire another yacht while his own was under repair his measure of damages for loss of use would be the sum paid for the hire of a comparable yacht, less any expenses which would be common to both yachts.

PERSONAL INJURY AND DEATH

Clearly the skipper of a yacht has a liability to those on board to take reasonable care in all the circumstances and not to expose crew or passengers to unnecessary danger. So far as a yacht's policy of insurance is concerned, it is worth remembering that this is a contract of indemnity for the insured alone, and does not automatically entitle any third party to compensation unless it can be shown that the skipper/owner himself was at fault and that none of the defences or partial defences to negligence (dealt with below) applied.

LIABILITY IN THE TEACHING OF SAILING

Instructors, or the principals, of a teaching establishment or club giving teaching have to consider the safety of the craft which they use, the safety of the system of teaching and supervision of students, and their liability to those whom they teach.

Broadly speaking, a person (other than an employer) cannot be held legally responsible for his actions unless he fails in his duty to take care to avoid causing "reasonably foreseeable injury" to others. What is "reasonably foreseeable" will be judged on the circumstances of each case, but it will be a material factor that sailing has certain inherent risks, and the duty of care must be seen in that context. For example, rough weather is one of the inherent risks of sailing.

The degree to which negligence is involved in any accident occurring in rough weather will depend upon the facts. Deliberately to ignore forecasts of dangerously rough weather could constitute negligence, but otherwise the possibility of adverse conditions has to be accepted by a volunteer undergoing instruction.

It will be apparent that it is possible for a club involved in teaching to be sued for negligence, if a duty of care is found to exist, and it is reasonable to expect a sailing teaching establishment to extend its insurance to cover regular voluntary instructors; but instructors should check to make sure this is done as a club, the members could be shown collectively to have committed an act which can be proved to be negligent.

Employer's Liability

As between an employer and an employee there are two principles of law. The first is that an employer is liable in law for the negligent act of his employee (acting within the scope of his employment) irrespective of any fault on the employer's part (this is known as vicarious liability).

The second principle is that an employer has a legal obligation towards his employee to provide him with safe working conditions. i.e an employee must not be faced with avoidably hazardous conditions or work (this is known as employer's liability).

Both risks are very usual ones, and the employer can (indeed must) insure against them.

Voluntary Instructors

A voluntary instructor who is himself injured in the course of an activity is in a position a good deal worse than that of an employee. He is outside the scope of the principle of employer's liability. Therefore, he should consider insuring himself for personal injury.

He should perhaps even more importantly, consider the possibility of a claim being made against him by a pupil who has been injured by his acts. Should he be proved negligent a court could award damages against him, and these, since he has held himself out as being competent to teach, may well be quite substantial. The RYA provides a special third party insurance policy for qualified instructors to cover them against legal claims for death or personal injury.

Adult Pupils

A person cannot generally complain of injury or damage if he or she voluntarily accepted the risk of such injury or damage. He or she should perhaps insure against personal accident because, in any action for negligence against an Instructor, the Court will, even if negligence is accepted, probably find that any damage is minimised by that act of voluntarily turning up for instruction. Such an act implies that certain risks are accepted. The ordinary perils of the sea, the risk of being allocated an unseaworthy boat or one that becomes unseaworthy, and the risk of sailing in unknown waters are clearly present and could be argued to have been voluntarily accepted.

Training accidents of the most obvious kind, such as might be sustained to the skull during an accidental gybe; to a hand during a collision between two heavy training dinghies; or to a back while hauling a dinghy up a beach are all part and parcel of the obvious risks that face novice pupils, and which do not need to be pointed out specifically to each one. By the same token, however, the dangers of drowning and hypothermia facing a capsized dinghy sailor arising from a sudden change in the weather or following the withdrawal of safety boat cover are something that are not evident to novices, and thus the instructor must have pointed out such dangers if he wishes the court to find that the risks were willingly accepted. An adult pupil should also ensure, if he or she is in a borrowed yacht, that the yacht's insurance policy indemnifies both the skipper and helmsman under instruction against third party claims.

As a matter of comment, the standard Householder's Policy which normally contains cover against third party claims, might well cover a person who has such a policy in these circumstances because sailing, not being one of the "dangerous" sports, is unlikely to be specifically excluded.

Young Pupils

The law imposes a special duty of care on adults, particularly adult instructors, responsible for children and young persons.

A child will never be held by a court to have voluntarily assumed a risk, unless he is of sufficient age and intelligence to appreciate the risk in question.

So each case will turn on its particular facts and it will be a matter of degree as to the duty of care. The duty of care towards a child is that to be expected of a reasonably conscientious parent towards his own child in the circumstances. While such a parent will not be totally indifferent towards potential danger neither will he be overprotective.

Bearing all this in mind, there remains the question of the establishment's or instructor's liability for a minor when he or she is not physically under sailing instruction. The situation can be envisaged where children, with their known propensity for getting into trouble, could cause a school, a club or an instructor (for the time being "in loco parentis") problems not associated at all with sailing tuition in, for example, "off duty" time. What might be considered unlikely situations (such as a physical argument with another pupil, deliberate damage or vandalism) perhaps find no true place in a discussion of a teaching situation but may nevertheless arise.

Because the law requires a high standard of care towards minors even in such a case, an injured pupil might well have a cause of action against the school or the club (or an individual instructor) but again a negligent failure to provide adequate supervision must be proved. It is sensible, therefore, for a teaching establishment or club to take advice when setting up, and from time to time, on these issues.

In a teaching situation, a boat being used for instruction is usually no different from a privately owned yacht or dinghy. All those utilising craft for this purpose should bear in mind that full disclosure of the particular use of the craft must be made to insurers, since the craft will obviously be used by the inexperienced and, as with the learner driver, the inherent risks are greater than if the helmsman were highly experienced.

LIABILITY OF INDIVIDUAL RACE OFFICERS

Most clubs are unincorporated bodies composed of individuals and under those circumstances a member cannot take legal action against the club. Hence members' liability to each other is not covered by insurance unless a "member to member" liability to each other is included in the policy. This helps to protect the race officer and the competing club member in case of legal action between the two.

Any intending race officer would be wise to investigate exactly what insurance arrangements have been made by the club for his protection.

That having been said, it is a most important defence in an action for negligence that the other party is a volunteer. If he voluntarily enters into any activity involving risk he generally cannot complain of injury or damage.

However, very different considerations apply in the case of young people. In the section on instruction we have discussed this point but, where races are organised for youngsters, they themselves may not have considered the risks involved, and a club faced with a claim under those circumstances might be unable to raise the defence of "Volenti" i.e. the assumption that all risks were voluntarily assumed by the youngster.

Club officers must take the view that they are in "loco parentis" and must take very much more care in organising races and events for young sailors than for adults.

There is no reason for a club to require that youngsters can only sail if their parents are in or around the club premises, so long as certain sensible precautions are taken.

The standard of care which a Race Officer would be expected by a court to show, in order to refute an allegation of negligence, would be such care towards a child under his charge as would be exercised by a reasonably careful parent who applies his mind to conditions of home life, and who also has as many children under his care as that Race Officer.

This, in reality, means that no more has to be done than would be "reasonable" in the particular circumstances. There is no formula for deciding what is "reasonable". If a club adopts a "buoyancy aid rule" for young sailors, does its best to ensure adequate safety boat cover during races, does not start races or practice sessions where conditions are particularly difficult or dangerous, and has a sensible arrangement for checking the boats out from the beach and in again then it has probably done all that a reasonably careful parent in that situation would do.

As we have explained above in the context of sailing instructors, a Race Officer is not expected to be a watch-dog or a disciplinarian; if a young person suffers an accident as a result of his own disobedience of a club rule, then, so long as the club is able to show that it takes its own rules reasonably seriously and makes reasonable attempts to enforce them, liability will probably not attach where an accident has occurred as a result of a breach of such rules by the young person injured.

DEFENCES TO NEGLIGENCE

The types of defence to an action for negligence are numerous, and indeed the use of the term "defence" is open to different interpretations. In this context we shall treat it as any ground for claiming non-liability or reduced liability for a claim for damages made by a party claiming damages for some injury.

Non-Liability

As in most civil law situations, the burden of proving a case rests on the plaintiff, the standard of proof being that of the balance of probabilities.

To show that a defendant is liable for damages, the plaintiff in an action for negligence has to satisfy the court as to the three elements of his claim - namely:-

(i) duty of care
(ii) breach of that duty
(iii) damage resulting from that breach.

(i) No Duty of Care

The question as to whether a person owes a duty of care to another is not always immediately obvious; for our purposes however we can take the definition of Lord Atkin, (Donaghue -v- Stephenson (1929)) that "you must take reasonable care to avoid acts or omissions which you can reasonably foresee would be likely to injure your neighbour (i.e. any) person who is so closely and directly affected by my act that I ought reasonably to have him in contemplation as being so affected when I am directing my mind to the acts or omissions which are called into question").

The situation often arises where a person may be injured by the result of an act of another who owes him no duty of care. Thus a trespasser on private or club property, or a person wrongfully interfering with a boat in a dangerous state, cannot complain of injury since the owner of the property or boat owes no duty of care except to those who are expressly or impliedly authorised by him.

(ii) No Breach of Duty

The duty to take reasonable care to avoid damaging another's person or property is not, of course, an absolute duty. Many instances will come to mind where an accident may occur in a harbour, or in the course of a race, where it would be possible for an observer to apportion "blame" in the sense of causation, but where a court would not apportion blame since the error of judgment, or chain of circumstances resulting in the incident, does not amount to negligence.

A relatively common cause of damage in mooring areas is a yacht breaking adrift and striking another as she drifts on the wind or tide. To the layman it may seem that the facts of the matter speak for themselves, and that the owner of the yacht, or whoever was responsible for the broken mooring, must be liable. That is, however, not always the case; it is possible for a latent defect in a chain, or a storm of exceptional severity, to cause a yacht to break free in circumstances where, if the owner can show that he took reasonable care (e.g. by having his mooring examined each year, and having tackle of sufficient strength to cope with normally expected weather conditions) he will escape liability.

In a recent County Court case a motor yacht manoeuvring slowly in a marina struck a moored yacht when the remote control gear apparatus stuck in forward gear. The Defendant was able to show that he took reasonable care to service his installation on a regular basis. The Defendant's expert surveyor investigating the incident was unable to recreate the fault without first removing the gearbox cover and "helping" the cable to jump its guide. The Court took the view that this was a one-in-a-million chance from which no liability arose.

The fact that a collision is caused by a mechanical failure will only be a defence if the failure arose through no fault of the Defendant. In the case of The Merchant Prince (1892) a collision occurred as a result of the steering wheel becoming jammed. The probable cause of the jamming was that the chain connecting the steering gear with the rudder had been allowed to become loose, causing kinks in the linkage. It was then held that the Defendant had been negligent in failing to maintain the steering gear properly and was thus liable.

An argument which is often relied upon in collision cases is the plea that the act alleged to be negligent was committed solely in the "agony of the moment". Proof of this can override the general obligation to exercise the due care and skill which is expected of a seaman when he finds himself in a dangerous situation. For this defence to succeed, the defendant must be able to show that he had no time to think of imminent danger, and no time to form a deliberate and properly calculated alternative plan of action to avoid the critical situation with which he was suddenly confronted.

Circumstances will often arise in the course of a yacht or dinghy race where a helmsman has to make snap decisions, where a wrong decision or momentary inattention may have serious consequences. It will not always follow that an error of judgment or loss of concentration will be considered "negligent" by a Court. In an unreported County Court case involving a collision between two Lasers running in close pursuit in a race at the Hillingdon Sailing Base, where the leading Laser capsized and the helmsman of the following took insufficient avoiding action, damaging the capsized craft, it was held that this error of judgment did not amount to negligence (even though he was in the wrong under the rules, and retired promptly).

(iii) No Damage

It goes without saying that the Plaintiff must show he has suffered damage of some sort. While the damage need not necessarily be material, it must be such that a monetary value can be put on it. The loss of use of a yacht can be valued by reference to the cost of chartering a replacement, but the loss of an opportunity to gain personal satisfaction and prestige by winning an important race or series is probably too remote and ill-defined to be evaluated. It is also essential to liability that the defendant's wrongdoing should have caused the plaintiff's damage. The case of The Douglas (1882) illustrates this concept. A ship sank in the Thames solely as a result of the negligence of those in charge of her, and became a wreck obstructing the river. Without any further fault on the part of the defendant, the wreck was struck by the plaintiff's ship which was damaged. It was held that this was not the consequence of the original negligence, which had ceased to be relevant after the sinking, the defendant's negligence having "exhausted" itself at the time of the original incident, and the wreck thereafter being properly marked. Questions of "remoteness" and "causation" are notoriously difficult concepts (especially in marine cases). Specialist legal advice will nearly always be needed where a claim arises.

Volenti Non Fit Injuria

The meaning of this legal maxim is that one who willingly participates in a risky activity cannot complain if injured.

Thus an experienced yachtsman, who appreciates and accepts the intrinsic risks of yacht racing, can reasonably be expected to foresee that damage or loss may be occasioned as a result of starting a race, or sailing a particular course in a certain type of vessel in bad weather, and may even be deemed negligent himself in so doing. On the other hand, a crew member known to be inexperienced will not foresee the possible harm, nor could he reasonably be expected to, and would not necessarily be negligent in undertaking the risks. In such case both the skipper and the organising club may owe a duty of care to that crew member and a defence of "volenti" will fail.

Although consent is normally implied by the courts in all properly conducted sports, no one is deemed to consent to a deliberate foul. While one has to accept the risk of damage or injury arising from an honest mistake, momentary carelessness or an error of judgment, a deliberate act outside the rules resulting in injury or damage will usually be actionable.

Where children are involved, the Courts will take a pragmatic view as to whether the child, in all the circumstances and having regard to the nature of the risk, can sensibly be held to have consented to the risk. Below the age of 13 or 14 the onus of proof will be on the defendant to show that a child, particularly if inexperienced in the sport, knew of the risks.

Contributory Negligence

The Law Reform (Contributory Negligence) Act 1945 provides that where any person suffers damage as the result partly of his own fault and partly of the fault of another he is entitled to recover damages with such a reduction as the Court thinks just and equitable having regard to his share in the responsibility for the damage.

In practice the concept of contributory negligence is not a defence, but is pleaded where the Defendant feels that the Plaintiff has to accept some of the blame for an occurrence or has by his own behaviour exacerbated the damage caused.

In the same context as "volenti", contributory negligence will not apply to an action brought on behalf of a minor.

Act of God

Act of God can be defined as an operation of natural forces which is so unexpected that any consequence arising from it must be regarded as too remote to be a foundation for legal liability. It need not be spectacular, such as lightning or flooding; even a rat gnawing through a wire has been held to be an Act of God.

Inevitable Accident

This is defined as an accident not avoidable by any such precaution as a reasonable man, doing such an act there and then, could be expected to take. In the context of an action for negligence, it really amounts to a more specific means of denying a breach of the duty of care. In truth all accidents can be avoided, so long as adequate precautions are taken, but the law will never impose a higher standard of care than could be expected of a reasonable man under the circumstances in question.

LIMITATION OF LIABILITY

Under the terms of the Merchant Shipping Act 1894 Section 503 (as amended by the Merchant Shipping Act 1976) a yacht owner would not be liable for damage above a sum equivalent to £40.00 per ton where damage to property was involved or £120.00 per ton for loss of life or personal injury subject to a minimum notional tonnage of 300 tons. Hence the owner or skipper of the yacht causing personal injury (for example) would never need, because of the limitation rules, to pay out more than 300 x £120.00 regardless of the damages that the court may have wished to award.

After 1st December 1986 new legislation, set the national minimum tonnage at a much higher level, linked to International Units of Account.

For property damage an owner/skipper will not be able to limit below 83,333 Units of Account. For loss of life or personal injury the platform will be 166,667 International Units of Account.

Perhaps, the most obvious consequence of these rules for pleasure sailors is that full damage for catastrophically serious injuries sustained at sea will not be fully recoverable from the negligent party.

From a historical view point the concept of allowing a ship owner to limit his liability arose as a matter of public policy in order to protect international trade. The United Kingdom, along with most other trading countries in the world, bases its rules for determining a ship owner's limited liability on the Brussels Convention relating to Limitation of Liability of Owners of Seagoing Ships 1957. Since that particular Convention the value of ships, cargoes, port installations, like everything else, has risen considerably as also have claims arising from marine casualties. It was therefore felt that the limits imposed by the 1957 Convention were too low. For this reason, together with a need to change the regulations to make it more certain that the relevant parties could be assured of their entitlement to limit liability, a new convention was brought into effect in 1976.

Under the 1957 Convention the owner of a seagoing ship was the party entitled to limit liability. The 1976 Convention extended the right to limit to salvors, persons for whose act, neglect or default the ship owner or salvor is responsible and any insurer of liability for claims subject to limitation in accordance with the rules of the 1976 Convention. These provisions are contained in Article 1 of the Convention, which clarifies the meaning of the words "ship owner" and "salvor". The reason for the amendment regarding salvors is to enable them to limit their liability in circumstances similar to the case of the "Tojo Maru" (1971) in which it was decided by the House of Lords that a salvor could not limit his liability in respect of damage caused to a vessel where a diver caused an explosion by negligently firing a bolt through plating into a tank on the vessel which had not be freed of gas. His employers where not able to limit liability by reference to the tonnage of the salvage tug because the diver was not working on board the tug at the time the explosion occurred. The 1976 amendment enables a salvor to claim the right of limitation when operating on board a ship in respect of which salvage services are being rendered.

One of the most significant effects of the 1976 Convention is that the personal "fault or privity" rule has been abolished in favour of a new standard for rating the limitation. Under the previous rule, a ship owner could not claim limitation if it could be shown by a plaintiff that the loss or damage complained of was caused by the ship owner directly rather than by a captain, helmsman, engineer etc acting on behalf of the ship owner. The 1976 Convention replaces the concept of" fault or privity" with the new provision that a ship owner will lose his right to limit liability only "if it is proved that the loss resulted from his personal act or omission, committed with the intent to cause such loss, or recklessly and with knowledge that such loss would probably result".

This new wording effectively gives the ship owner very much more protection since in future a plaintiff will have to show that there has been some element of maliciousness, and indeed that it was the personal maliciousness of the person attempting to limit liability. Therefore to breach the limitation provision, it must be proved that the act or omission was a personal act or omission of the person liable, and furthermore that it was committed recklessly with knowledge that the loss that did occur would probably result.

At the time of writing there has been no judicial interpretation in the English Courts of the new provisions although it is thought unlikely that a plaintiff will be able to prove in any realistic circumstances that the owner or helmsman of a yacht should not be entitled to limit his liability.

JURISDICTION OF COURT

Collision between yachts or ships may occur on the high seas or in foreign waters as much as in British territorial waters, and may involve a vessel or vessels of another nationality. Generally a legal action can always be brought in the country under whose flag the defendant vessel is sailing, but this can lead to delay and expense, and for a citizen of the United Kingdom it is always preferable to bring an action in their own country. The British courts will allow collision actions to be brought if the guilty vessel, irrespective of its nationality, is in a British port at the time when the action is brought. This is the case even if the collision occurs on the high seas or in foreign territorial waters. Similar rules apply in the French, German and Italian courts and in cases involving collisions between merchant ships it is not unusual for the procedural and jurisdictional dispute to be as hard fought as the substantive action.

Where a yacht owner intends to bring proceedings against another vessel or her owner, Section 8 of the Maritime Conventions Act 1911 provides that any action must be commenced within two years from the date when the damage or loss or injury occurred (or salvage services were re-endorsed). This is in contrast to the general law which allows six years for civil claims (or three years for personal injury).

Deliberate acts

Very occasionally a yachtsman may suffer injury through the deliberate criminal act of another person. Provided the injury occurs in the United Kingdom (including on board a British ship), is at least moderately serious (is worth more than £500 in damages) and was reported promptly to the police, payment in compensation for injuries (on the same scale as those recoverable in a civil court) will be paid by the Criminal Injuries Compensation Board from State funds. No conviction is needed, but a claim should be made promptly.

CHAPTER 6

SALVAGE, TOWAGE AND LOSS OF PROPERTY AT SEA

INTRODUCTION AND DEFINITIONS

Salvage is a voluntary service not in performance of any legal or official duty which, when a vessel is in danger at sea, saves the vessel, contributes to the safety of such a vessel, its gear or its cargo or contributes to the safety of the lives of those within such a vessel.

It is true that salvage is very often carried out under a Salvage Contract but this is not a prerequisite.

The underlying principles governing a salvage claim are thus:-

(a) The service must be rendered to a legally-recognised subject of salvage, that is to say, to vessels, their gear, cargo and merchandise, wreck, or freight at risk;
(b) The service must be voluntary and not under some pre-arranged contract;
(c) The subject of the salvage must be in danger;
(d) The service must be successful;
(e) The service must be performed in tidal waters and not within a harbour authority's area of jurisdiction (MSA 1894 S.546 and S.742).

Before a rescuer can assert a claim to salvage against the owner he must show that what he has saved is "wreck". The definition of "wreck" is a ship or (whether or not the ship itself is lost) its gear, equipment or cargo.

"Flotsam", "Jetsam", "Lagan" and "Derelict" are all within the definition of "wreck".

"Flotsam" exists where a vessel is lost and the wreckage floats on the sea.

"Jetsam" is material cast into the sea to lighten ship.

"Lagan" is material cast into the sea but buoyed to mark its position.

"Derelict" is property, whether ship or cargo, abandoned at sea without hope or intention then of returning to it.

Under the Sea Fisheries Act 1883 all boats, gear, nets, floats, etc. of fishing boats, whether marked or not, fall within the definition of "wreck".

Suppose that a navigation buoy comes adrift and is safely taken ashore, since this is not part of the equipment of any ship, it is not "wreck" in law and therefore cannot be the subject of salvage.

Similarly, if a high tide carries away a yacht club's launching trolleys and they are later rescued by someone (or if the club's racing buoys come adrift and are found) the Secretary should make no concession to a rescuer claiming salvage. Whilst a rescuer may have a moral claim to reward, in law he is simply the finder of someone else's property and is obliged to return it. He has no kind of nautical "lien" (a right to hold another's property against satisfaction of a claim) over it.

Thus, if the finder of property could, by taking reasonable steps, discover the identity of the loser, but fails to do so and keeps the property for his own use, he may well be guilty of "theft by finding".

The importance of this is that the finder of "wreck" is required by law to hand it over to the Receiver of Wreck. In practice, this official will usually be the local Customs or Coastguard Officer. There are penalties for failing to hand over "wreck" as there are for hiding, defacing or taking it away. The Receiver can, in fact, obtain a warrant from a local Justice of the Peace to carry out a search of premises where it is suspected that a salvor has hidden "wreck".

When "wreck", be it an unclaimed dinghy, sail covers, or any other ship's gear, comes into the possession of the Receiver he has a duty to post up a notice, within 48 hours, at the local Customs House, describing the property and any distinguishing marks it bears. In case of valuable items a further notice must go to Lloyd's of London, but if the article is of very small value, or is perishable or damaged, it may be sold and the proceeds retained for the owner.

The owner may normally prove his claim to the property within one year and get it back (or the proceeds of sale of the property) but he may have to meet expenses and a possible salvage claim.

The Receiver also has the power to "suppress plundering or disorder where a vessel is wrecked or stranded" and it is an offence for any one to board such a vessel without permission from the owner or the Receiver.

Ashore, if one voluntarily puts oneself at risk and expense to save another's property, (say his house or his motor car) this does not impose any legal obligation on the owner to repay the salvor. Neither does he get a "lien" on the property saved unless he can prove a contract of employment, either express or implied, under which he could make a claim to be rewarded. The same considerations do not apply at sea.

It is the equitable principle of remunerating private and individual services, meritorious in their nature, which forms the foundation of salvage in accordance with the rules of simple justice. The protection of life and of maritime property at sea is of paramount importance and is therefore encouraged by the courts.

NO CURE - NO PAY

Next to voluntariness, another principle of a salvage award is that the property or part of it must be saved. Unless there is a special contract to pay, independently of the ultimate safety of the property, the principle remains "no cure - no pay".

DANGER

Is a third aspect of a salvage service. The vessel involved or someone on it must be in real danger.

Perhaps this rule makes salvage suspect amongst amateur sailors, for, having recovered from the misery of seasickness and exhaustion, a yachtsman may sometimes forget an agreement readily made a few hours earlier when he and his craft were in need of aid.

The test really is, would a prudent mariner in the circumstances existing have asked for help ?

The burden of proving that real (though not necessarily immediate) danger existed is upon those who claim as salvors. The danger can be proved to exist not only from the state of the salved vessel or her position (e.g. on a lee shore) but because of the condition of the crew or the master's ignorance of the locality or his lack of skill. Also, the salvor would be entitled to say that the conduct of those on board in giving signals of distress or accepting help was evidence of such danger. Persons induced by ambiguous signals to go to the help of any vessel which, in fact, is damaged or in danger, are entitled to claim as salvors.

SALVAGE SERVICES

Small boat owners should realise that it can be salvage to set in motion the steps to bring help to a boat or (just possibly) coming alongside and giving advice or information, which would enable it to avoid a local danger. No doubt, the common advice to yachtsmen to use their own warps when taking a tow is, in part, based on the fact that it has been held a valid salvage service to supply tackle to a vessel in need of it. The salvor need not do anything as dramatic as putting out a fire or manning the pumps. Salvage services include towing, pilotage, navigating, or standing by a boat. Taking off any equipment or taking a passenger ashore could also be salvage.

It has even happened that a pilot contracted to perform a pilotage service has acted over and above the call of duty and voluntarily to the extent of bringing his actions within the realm of salvage services independently of his contractual duties as a pilot. In the case of The Sandefjord (1953) 2 LL 557, the master of a ship aground on the Goodwins in charge of a pilot took the pilot's advice to use the ship's own kedge anchor rather than accept offers of assistance from tugs. The Court held that the pilot's advice amounted to salvage services; not only did he take a personal professional risk in giving this advice, but he also relieved the ship's owner of a large salvage award for tug assistance.

Floating a stranded vessel (or raising one which is sunken) or saving a "derelict" or "wreck" are readily recognised as salvage.

Hence, removing a vessel from a dangerous adjacent fire may be salvage just as much as putting out a fire upon the vessel itself, and so indeed may services which save her from being plundered by thieves.

SALVAGE OF LIFE

Although there is a statutory requirement under S.6 of the Maritime Conventions Act 1911 to render assistance to any vessel in distress and to save life, it is possible for the saving of that life to be the subject of a salvage claim.

However, in the absence of some specific agreement, this cannot be sustained unless some property was also saved out of the proceeds from which a salvage claim could be met. Therefore no claim for "life salvage" would be payable if the crew of a yacht were saved, but the yacht and all their possessions were lost. In such a case there might be a discretionary award payable out of public funds to the salvors.

TOWAGE SERVICES

Towage is a contract for expediting the voyage of a vessel when nothing more is needed than "accelerating her progress". Hence, in the usual case, no claim can be made for salvage by a tug towing a salved vessel under a contract of towage.

The tug and towed vessel are legally one ship. If a vessel is being towed under a towage contract it will usually be the case (unless your vessel is a "wreck" or there is an agreement to the contrary) that the tug is the servant of the tow.

This rule avoids confusion over possible divided responsibility. The tug has a duty to use reasonable care and it would seem that, if orders given by the tow were clearly wrong, it would be the duty of the tug to warn of the consequences. However, if there is a collision, liability may well rest on the towed vessel and if, for example, the tug is not carrying proper lights it may be the tow which will be held responsible for the damage occasioned thereby.

A TUG-OWNER'S RESPONSIBILITIES

A tug owner impliedly holds himself out as being competent to undertake such work. This is an ordinary rule of contract. However, it cannot be implied that the tug owner holds himself out at being competent to carry out the work under any circumstances. Certain hazards may relieve him from responsibility so that the initial contract of towage is discharged. If a tug owner has not been told of difficulties or dangers which are serious enough to make it unjust to expect that the service should be undertaken at the usual towage rates, then the towage contract might well be discharged and the service, if still continuing, could be treated as a salvage service.

During performance of a contract of towage, the weather may deteriorate and the yacht being towed may become endangered through no fault of the tug. The tug may then render services in the nature of salvage, over and above what might reasonably have been held to be within the intention of the towage contract. If the yacht is brought to safety, the towage contract may be deemed to have been superseded by the right to a salvage award.

Strict proof of such a transformation of the situation is normally required by the Courts. A small departure from the way in which the towage was to be performed will certainly not convert towage into salvage services. If lack of skill or equipment on the part of the tug materially contributed to the danger experienced by the towed vessel then the owner or crew of the tug will not be entitled to a salvage award even though there may also have been negligence by the towed vessel.

SALVAGE AND THE PUBLIC SERVICES

Confusion exists about the Lifeboat Service's, the Coastguards', Harbour Masters' and other public servants' right to salvage. The RNLI has life-saving as its main object and the Institution makes no claim for salvage. With few exceptions it does not actually employ the life-boat crews. These men are volunteers, paid no wages, but rewarded on a negotiated scale when they use a life-boat provided that they are not claiming salvage. If the life-boat can safely be spared from normal duty and if no other suitable craft is available, the crew may then decide to use the life-boat for a salvage service and the Institution does not control this decision provided its regulations are complied with.

If a claim be made and an award granted the Institution then claims against the crew all the costs of borrowing its life-boat.

Since the award in favour of a life-boat crew is normally the "crew's share" only and does not include the "ship's share" the total award may well be only half of what would be payable to a commercial salvor.

Coastguards, Harbour Masters and other public servants can only claim salvage for work outside their official duties and claims are rarely made.

Recent claims against yacht owners by both the Royal Navy and the French Navy also serve as a reminder that assistance should only be sought, and offers of towage accepted, in cases of serious need. It has indeed been specifically held in court that state-owned ships have an equal entitlement to a fair and reasonable reward for salvage.

SALVAGE AWARDS

In assessing the amount of an award for a salvage service, a Court will look at all the factors, i.e. the value of each vessel involved in the operation and of the property saved, the danger to the vessels and to the salvors, and the expense, skill and time involved.

The status of the salvor, professional or amateur, would be considered and also the conduct and skill displayed by the salvage team.

Very rarely will the award be more than 50% of the salved value, and in most cases very much less.

The yacht skipper and his crew should therefore take careful note of all such circumstances, show themselves as much as possible in control of the situation, (e.g. by using their own gear) and endeavour to see that independent corroboration (e.g. from weather reports, charts or a well-kept log) is available in case of dispute.

In general salvage awards, in the rare cases where disputes remain unsettled, and come to Court, tend to be modest in relation to the value of the vessel. Since the amount of the award is based on the value of the vessel as salved, the owner or insurer must certainly be better off than if she had been lost.

If dispute arises after the vessel is saved, the yachtsman's proper course will be to consult his solicitor and his insurers and leave negotiations to them. Indeed, most insurance policies require immediate written notice of any accident or of any claim and demand that no negotiations, payments, settlements, admission or repudiation of any claim is given without the written consent of the insurers.

So far as the likely amount of the award will be, we can do no better than to examine three cases involving pleasure craft which reached the court in the absence of an agreed settlement.

In the case of the Ocean Hound (1950) this seventy-two foot twin-screw wooden motor yacht went aground near Dungeness on a shingle bank, near an old wreck and adjacent to old sea defence works. The wind was a light north-westerly and the tide was ebbing. The Dungeness lifeboat arrived to assist and refloated her, taking her to a safe anchorage a mile offshore. The value of the salved yacht was £1,500, and the whole service took one and a half hours. The court accepted that the weather might have deteriorated and that the yacht had been rescued from a position of considerable potential, if not actual, danger. The services rendered were easy for qualified and well-equipped men, but they should be encouraged to salvage property from danger. The court awarded a sum of 10% of the salved value together with fuel, oil and launching expenses of the life-boat.

In the case of the Guernsey Coast (1950) a motor vessel had received short but helpful advice as to where to find a better anchorage when in bad weather she was dragging on Margate Sand. The judge awarded £250 on a salved value of £84,000.

In the case of the Evaine the court awarded £750 on a salved value of £3,000 for going alongside and successfully fighting a fire after the yacht had been abandoned by her crew. The fishing boat undertaking the salvage faced a "very real risk" of explosion in the circumstances which justified the award of 25%.

LIEN

We discuss in Chapter 7 that a salvor has a maritime lien on property salved. This is a right to arrest the vessel even if it has changed hands and to sell it to meet his claims. Since this lien is good security, the salvor will not normally be allowed to retain the rescued ship and prevent the owner from dealing with it. He will only be allowed to do this in the case of a "derelict" or where there are some special circumstances endangering the security of the wreck. Where a salvor has unnecessarily retained possession of a yacht or refused access to the owner, this will be taken into account by the court in assessing the salvage claim, and he may even lose any right to an award.

Apart from the claim against the ship, the salvor has also a personal claim against the owner if he be unable to get his award satisfied from the proceeds of sale of the vessel.

SALVAGE AGREEMENTS

A form of Salvage Agreement is set out below. It is based on a far more elaborate form (Lloyd's Open "Standard Form") which provides for an award in the event of success, declaring the services to be salvage services and that the salvor gets a licence to use the vessel's gear. It is usually wise not to fill in any sum of remuneration but, even if done, this could still be the subject of arbitration as having been obtained under duress.

A Salvage Agreement involves the salvor bargaining for a reward beforehand. There are various implied conditions in such an agreement:

(i) the property is actually in danger;
(ii) the salvor is not already under a duty arising from another contract (such as a towage contract);
(iii) the salvor is not acting in an official position;

(iv) unless there is a term to the contrary in the Agreement, the services must be successful - no cure, no pay;
(v) the sum agreed must be paid out of the proceeds of the property saved;
(vi) the salvor has a lien on such property;
(vii) the Agreement is made in good faith, all material facts having been disclosed.

DAMAGE BY THE SALVORS

The yacht being salved often suffers further damage. The salvor may lose any right to reward if he is guilty of wrongful or criminal misconduct (e.g. wrongfully preventing the yacht's skipper from returning on board or by the theft of gear). The salvor may also lose the right to reward if he is grossly negligent by, for example, bringing the yacht into dangers at least as great as those from which he sought to rescue her. Even if she is ultimately saved, the original salvage services have not "contributed" to that success. There have, however, been occasions when a yacht has called upon salvage services, (e.g. for the provision of an additional anchor from the shore) and she is then actually saved through some other completely different cause. This assistance, though unproductive of benefit, is entitled to reward.

CONTRACTS MADE UNDER STRESS

If a yacht is in difficulties, the skipper will clearly be unlikely in many cases to be able to arrange a written agreement. If he feels that he can get her safely to harbour with the help of a tow of convenience, he should try to arrange a towage contract, but if those coming to his help insist on working on a salvage basis he should then ensure that the services are agreed to be "salvage services" under the normal Lloyd's open "Standard Form" upon the principle of "No Cure No Pay" and settle the maximum remuneration in the event of success.

Under the circumstances envisaged he should at least ensure that his crew are witnesses to what is arranged orally and that all the points are covered.

A SIMPLE FORM OF SALVAGE AGREEMENT

"NO CURE - NO PAY"
(Incorporating Lloyd's Open Form)

On board the Yacht Date
IT IS HEREBY AGREED BETWEEN
for and on behalf of the Owners of the
(Hereinafter called "the Owners")

AND for and on behalf of
(hereinafter called "the Contractor")

1. That the Contractor will use his best endeavours to salve the and take her into
or such other place as may hereinafter be agreed or if no place is named or agreed to a place of safety.
2. That the services shall be rendered by the Contractor and accepted by the owner as salvage services upon the principle of "No Cure - No Pay" subject to the terms conditions and provisions (including those relating to Arbitration and providing of security) of the current Standard Form of Salvage Agreement approved and published by the Council of Lloyd's of London and known as Lloyd's Open Form.
3. In the event of success the Contractor's remuneration shall be £ or if no sum be mutually agreed between the parties or entered herein the same shall be fixed by arbitration in London in the manner prescribed in Lloyd's Open Form.
4. The Owners their servants and agents shall cooperate fully with the Contractor in and about the salvage including obtaining entry to the place named in Clause 1 hereof or the place of safety. The Contractor may make reasonable use of the vessel's machinery gear equipment anchors chains stores and other appurtenances during and for the purpose of the services free of expense but shall not unnecessarily damage abandon or sacrifice the same or any property the subject of this Agreement.
For and on behalf of the Owners of property to be salved

....

For and on behalf of the Contractor

....

Note Full copies of the Lloyd's Open Form Salvage Agreement can be obtained from the Salvage Arbitration Branch, Lloyd's of London, One Lime Street, London, EC3M 7HA. Tel: 071 623 7100, Ext. 5849, who should be notified of the services only when no agreement can be reached as to remuneration.

CHAPTER 7

LIEN AND ARREST

LIEN

A lien is defined as the right to retain in possession an item or chattel which belongs to another, until certain demands by the person in possession have been met by the owner; or in the case of maritime liens, to place an enforceable charge over a vessel.

A possessory lien is the right to retain a chattel until outstanding charges in respect of it have been cleared. Thus a repairer, or a marina (by prior contractual agreement), or a person involved in salvage services has a right to retain possession. Once he has lost possession (unless by fraud or duress) the lien is not revived by his retaking possession.

A statutory lien may arise where stores or equipment are delivered to a vessel and not paid for. In these circumstances the vessel itself can be sued and arrested by High Court or County Court action (see below).

A maritime lien is a form of charge which attaches to a vessel and which follows the vessel even when it is sold by the owner in whose hands the debt or liability first arose. Such a lien arises as a result of a claim for salvage service as discussed in Chapter 6, or a claim for damage occasioned by the vessel, and entitles the Court to arrest and, where appropriate, order the sale of the vessel.

Where the lien arises from damage done by the vessel, the plaintiff must show some negligence or want of due diligence by the skipper or owner. It should be noted that even if the owner has chartered the yacht or left it in the hands of a boat yard, then a lien will attach if the circumstances indicate that the person in control at the time of the incident was acting within his authority as granted by the owner and with the consent of the owner.

ARREST OF SHIPS

The International Convention on the Arrest of Seagoing Ships (Brussels 1952) and the Supreme Court Act 1981 lay down the circumstances in which a court may order the arrest of a vessel.

The following circumstances will entitle a person to maintain an action against not only the owner of a vessel but also the vessel itself :-

(a) Any claim to the possession or ownership of a ship or to the ownership of any claim therein;
(b) Any question arising between the co-owners of a ship as to

possession, employment or earnings of that ship;

(c) Any claim in respect of a mortgage of or charge on a ship or any share therein;

(d) Any claim for damage received by a ship;

(e) Any claim for damage done by a ship;

(f) Any claim for loss of life or personal injury sustained in consequence of any defect in a ship or in her apparel or equipment, or in consequence of the wrongful act, neglect or default of :-

  (i) the owners, charterers or persons in possession or control of a ship; or

  (ii) the master or crew of a ship, or any other person for whose wrongful act, neglect or default the owners, charterers or persons in possession or control of a ship are responsible, being an act, neglect or default in the navigation or management of the ship, or in the loading, carriage or discharge of goods on, in or from the ship.

(g) Any claim for loss of or damage to goods carried in a ship;

(h) Any claim arising out of any agreement relating to the carriage of goods in a ship or to the use or hire of a ship;

(i) Any claim in the nature of salvage;

(j) Any claim in the nature of towage;

(k) Any claim in the nature of pilotage;

(l) Any claim in respect of goods and materials supplied to a ship for her operation or maintenance.

(m) Any claim in respect of the construction, repair or equipment of a ship or in respect of dock charges or dues;

(n) Any claim by a master or member of the crew of a ship for wages (including any sum allotted out of wages or adjudged by a superintendent to be due by way of wages);

(o) Any claim by a master, skipper, charterer or agent in respect of disbursements made on account of a ship.

If, in the course of any proceedings in respect of a ship in a County Court or the High Court, the judge is satisfied that the vessel or property concerned may be removed out of the jurisdiction of the court before the plaintiff's claim is satisfied, he may issue a warrant for the arrest and detention of the vessel unless or until bail equal to the amount of the claim in the proceedings, together with a reasonable sum for costs, is deposited with the court.

If an improper arrest has been made the court will punish the person responsible for it by awarding costs against him and, in a flagrant case, ordering him to pay damages.

Once a vessel has been arrested and detained, or bail and security for costs has been lodged with the court, the case will then proceed to a hearing in the normal way.

CHAPTER 8

PUBLIC RIGHTS OF NAVIGATION

COASTAL AND TIDAL WATERS

Although the title to the bed of all navigable tidal waters is vested in the Crown (or in some person or corporation granted title by the Crown) there is a superior public right to navigate on those waters. This right extends as much to recreational craft as to merchant or naval craft and may only be interfered with by a specific and unambiguous Act of Parliament.

Thus every proposal to block a navigable tidal waterway, however rarely used, by (for instance) the construction of a bridge, barrage, dock or other construction is subject to the full Parliamentary process applied to all Private Bills, and consent will normally only be granted after full consideration and investigation of the balance of interest.

Whether an area of water is "navigable" or not will be a question of fact in all the circumstances of each case. In the case of Ilchester -v- Rashleigh (1889 61 LT 477) fishermen claimed a right to navigate over a small creek but, although there was evidence to show that there was sufficient water at the highest spring tides to allow small craft to navigate successfully, at most times there was insufficient rise of tide and the court held that in the absence of a "daily ebb and flow" there was no right of navigation.

Although the ebb and flow of tide is prima facie evidence of a waterway subject to a public right of navigation, whether a particular area is navigable depends very much upon its original nature. For instance a gravel or clay pit adjacent to tidal waters, into which a connecting channel has been dug, will not automatically be subject to a public right any more than a private creek or marina dug into saltings.

The right to navigate is in many ways similar to a right of way on a public highway. Just as on a highway one may stop and pass and re-pass at will, so owner of a vessel may anchor, run aground and sail back and forth. What he may not do without the consent of the fundus (bottom) owner is to establish a permanent mooring, although in law the distinction between anchoring and mooring is not as clear as it is to the yachtsman.

It has been established in the Courts that there is (except in very particular and unusual circumstances) no common law right to lay or maintain permanent moorings on another person's land without his permission. In Fowley Marine (Emsworth) Limited -v- Gafford (1967), the Court reached the conclusion that there is no Common Law right to lay or maintain permanent moorings, for it would - "be little less than fantastic that in the absence of Statute or proved local custom, the law should allow anyone navigating a ship or vessel, including every amateur yachtsman, to place bulky objects on another person's land without permission and to retain them there, presumably forever, as being an ordinary incident of navigation".

In this relatively modern case, other points were discussed which are of interest. Under the Limitation Act 1939, Section 4 (1), an action may be brought by the Crown "at any time before the expiration of sixty years" in order to recover rights which may have been taken or claimed by another person or organisation.

Ordinarily, uninterrupted dispossession of the true owner's land for a period of twelve years or more would effectively debar the true owner from claiming back that land, but as against the Crown the period is sixty years. But legal opinion is divided as to whether statute or case law has really established whether the act of laying and/or maintaining a permanent mooring can be an act or acts amounting to dispossession of land. It remains uncertain whether a landowner (including the Crown) is, after the appropriate period, really barred from bringing an action to recover the land upon which the mooring lies, largely because of the difficulty of exact definition of the area taken up by a mooring.

METHODS OF DISPOSSESSION

As already stated, there is no Common Law right to lay or maintain permanent moorings on another person's land without his permission. Such a right may possibly be acquired by "Lost Modern Grant" (a legal fiction which assumes that at some time a document granting the right may have been in existence but has now been lost or forgotten).

A person may also seek to prove "custom". This may best be briefly defined as "everybody has done it over many years and nobody has complained", and is limited to the benefit of local people.

The dispossession of the original owner's right may also be given by Statute. An example of this is the Water Act 1973 which gave to Regional Water Authorities considerable rights previously owned by others.

A person who lays or maintains a permanent mooring without permission may be a trespasser and accordingly (apart from the question of possession) be liable in damages to the owner of the sea-bed, river-bed etc. on or in which the mooring is placed.

A LAND OWNER'S RIGHT TO CLAIM RENT

In recent years, it is certainly true that a number of owners of "fundus" (i.e. land covered by water), (however they acquired title) have begun to insist upon their proven right to claim rent for that area of land covered either by ground tackle or "sinkers".

This is the natural outcome of the changing nature of the yachting scene and the increasing number of people requiring moorings. The level of rent or licence fee demanded by landlords obviously varies considerably from one area of the country to another. At the time of writing (1993) even the Crown Estate Commissioners valuations differ widely from the £10 per mooring per annum demanded in Scotland, to £90 per mooring per annum in some parts of Portsmouth Harbour.

CONSENTS REQUIRED FOR LAYING A MOORING IN TIDAL WATERS

The owner of the land covered by water can reasonably stop you from using his land upon which to lay a mooring. To lay a mooring without consent will normally be an act of trespass.

There are also other less obvious agencies who may need to be involved in the laying of moorings. These are the Department of Transport, the Crown Estate Commissioners and the Planning Authorities.

Department of Transport

Under Section 4 of the Coast Protection Act 1949 permission must be obtained from the Department of Transport before placing anything below high water mark which is, or may become, a danger to navigation. This includes mooring buoys.

The Merchant Shipping Act 1988 has to some extent amended this requirement by providing that where a harbour authority has the jurisdiction to license such works, and does so, the requirement to obtain consent from the Department of Transport will no longer apply.

Crown Estate Commissioners

Where land covered by tidal water apparently has no local owner it almost certainly belongs to the Crown. Hence the Crown Estate Commissioners (or the Duchy of Lancaster or Duchy of Cornwall) can exercise the rights of landlord and can withhold permission to lay a mooring until a rent has been agreed.

In practice the Commissioners will usually be only too pleased to grant a licence to lay moorings, whether to a harbour authority, a club, a fairways committee, or to an individual. It is the policy of the Commissioners to encourage the orderly development of moorings in the areas under their control, and their stated policy is to make reasonable charges to lessees of mooring areas. In practice this means that non-commercial mooring leases are made available to clubs, fairways committees and harbour authorities at a rate of between £10-£90 per mooring (1993 prices) depending on the region, level of demand, and the characteristics of the mooring area.

Planning Authorities

The laying of a mooring can sometimes be "development". Within the jurisdiction of a Planning Authority it is possible for that authority to restrain a person from laying a mooring by serving an Enforcement Notice. Local Government boundaries are defined, by the Local Government Act 1972 to a "medium" low water mark - effectively this low water mark is the point of low water at a date halfway between neap and spring tides. Such areas also include "accretions from the sea" and areas where the natural line of a watercourse has changed. The Town and Country Planning Act 1971 follows the same areas and Planning Authorities therefore have powers, generally speaking above that same tide level. Below it, the sea is not subject to planning control.

Some time ago the RYA asked Counsel to give an opinion on whether a Local Authority had power to serve an Enforcement Notice on a person who had laid a mooring, on the basis that it amounted to an unauthorised development.

Counsel confirmed what we have said about the seaward boundary of the Local Authority but he also discussed estuaries and arms of the sea. Whether an arm of the sea or a river is within the body of a county was considered in The Fagernes (1927). In the case of a narrow tidal stream, it would certainly lie within the local authority jurisdiction, but not in the case of a wide tidal river. The test was said to be whether a man on one shore could see what was done on the other. In the particular case it was probable that the river in question was within the parishes which formed the area of the administrative county for Local Government purposes. This is of course a question of fact in each case.

The onus of proof is on the person asserting that the land in question is within the county. The recipients of a Local Council planning notice are thus entitled to call on the Council to prove that the land covered by water is within the Council jurisdiction. If this proof is not forthcoming then the notice is void.

There are other aspects of the laying of moorings which might establish their permanence and therefore affect their status as "developments". For example, some types of moorings depend on concrete blocks or discs with an anchor bar to which the mooring line is fixed, dug into the mud. Where a mooring base merely rests on the hard bottom, it is less likely that the apparatus may amount to a "development" since it is the use of the land that is relevant.

Counsel also remarked that the Minister had taken the view that the mooring of vessels (not in the course of navigation) is an operation in, over and under land. There might however be cases where if the mooring was not fixed or embedded, and was moved from time to time, then the laying of the mooring would not be a development operation since the act in question involves solely the use of a chattel. Thus it would be perfectly permissible to anchor a boat and leave it where it could not be attached to a fixed mooring.

The mere fact that consent to lay a mooring has been obtained from the Harbour Authority or from the owners of the land did not, Counsel suggested, admit the need to obtain planning permission.

There are therefore two questions in each particular case which must be demonstrated by the facts :-

1. It must be established that the mooring is sufficiently permanent to be a true "development operation".
2. It must be established beyond doubt that the planning authority has jurisdiction over the piece of land covered by water in which the mooring has been laid, and over which the Council purports to have planning powers.

Harbours and Marinas

Harbour Authorities may derive their powers over harbour waters (which often extend further to seaward than may be realised) from Private Acts of Parliament or from the Harbours Act 1964 or from a mixture of both. One of the many powers which they have is that of dictating what moorings may be laid and where. Marina owners, dependent upon the size of the marina, derive their powers from either a Private Act of Parliament or from some lease or licence accorded to them from the Harbour Authority in which the marina may be situated.

They, naturally, have the right to prohibit the laying of unauthorised moorings, always supposing that there might be room to do so.

The public right of navigation also permits the yachtsman to fish (except where local Protective Orders are in force) or anchor or run aground, but not for the purposes of drying out for scrubbing or repainting, although this is a common and accepted practice.

RESTRICTIONS ON THE PUBLIC RIGHT OF NAVIGATION

Ministry of Defence

Many coastal areas are occupied by the Ministry of Defence (through the Property Services Agency) for gunnery or bombing practice, or as proving ranges. During firing times these ranges, which are normally delineated on the relevant Admiralty chart, are patrolled by MoD police who are entitled to request yachtsmen to keep clear of certain limits. While it is reasonable to comply with such requests so far as possible it must be stressed that in no case in the U.K. is there any range where the authorities have the right to exclude vessels passing from one side to another and taking no longer than is reasonably necessary to do so. The range byelaws on all such ranges controlling the right to navigate are carefully worded so as not to exclude the bona fide right to transit the range at any time, whether firing is scheduled or not, even for recreational craft taking no longer than is reasonably necessary to cross the area in question.

Harbour Authorities

Harbour Authorities of every harbour in the country are, quite rightly, given wide powers to control traffic entering, leaving, and moving within a harbour. What a Harbour Master cannot do is to exclude craft for any reason (except under the Dangerous Cargoes Act, and other specific legislation) or to prevent craft from moving except in the course of day-to-day control of traffic.

In the case of Pearn -v- Sargeant (1973) the Harbour Master at Looe purported to close the Harbour for the day to allow a regatta to take place and the owner of a craft within the harbour was prosecuted for failing to comply with the Harbour Master's directions. In the course of his judgment Lord Widgery CJ said, "The function of the Harbour Master under Section 52 (Harbours, Docks and Piers Clauses Act 1847) is to regulate the traffic; after all it is a public harbour where the public have a right to be and it is not the Harbour Master's function, as such, to keep them out. His function is to control and regulate them rather like a traffic policeman regulating traffic. Of course, there will be cases when he has to go beyond these simple functions; of course, there may be cases where necessity arises and he has to impose wider prohibitions for a particular time, but when that happens it is for consideration whether the directions he has given are reasonable for the emergency or circumstances which prompted them". In the circumstances the harbour authority's prosecution failed.

As with all public bodies, harbour authorities are under a duty implied by law to exercise their duties reasonably and only for purposes associated with their undertaking. Thus a recent proposal to site a Liquified Petroleum Gas tanker in a harbour as a permanent storage facility may well have been a reasonable use of the harbour, but the proposal to employ the Harbour Master's powers to give directions on a permanent basis so as to enforce a 500 metre safety radius around the ship was highly suspect at law and would probably have been unenforceable. Accordingly the scheme had to be withdrawn since no insurance company would entertain the risk unless they were sure that a safety radius could be lawfully imposed.

So far as harbour authority finances are concerned, authorities are entitled to levy dues, which pay for the enjoyment of the basic harbour works, and there are further charges, usually optional, to pay for the enjoyment of ancillary services. Dues are to a great extent in the nature of a tax, the amount payable being not directly referable to the service or services received by the user.

Under the terms of the Harbours Act 1964, a harbour authority is entitled to impose such dues as it thinks fit, subject only to a right of appeal by users to the Secretary of State for Transport. Under Section 31, written objections may be made as to the ship, passenger and goods dues imposed by a harbour authority at their harbour. An objector must be a person having a substantial interest in the question, or a body representative of such persons. Objections may be made on any of the following grounds:-

(a) that the charge ought not to be imposed at all
(b) that the charge ought to be imposed at a lower rate
(c) that, according to the circumstances of the case, ships, passengers or goods of a class specified in the objection ought to be excluded or reduced from the scope of the charge either generally or in circumstances so specified.

Where objections are made the Secretary of State will hold an inquiry, as a result of which he may approve the charge, or give relevant directions to the harbour authority to reduce or abolish the charge or otherwise satisfy the objection. In 1982 Weymouth and Portland Council introduced a substantial charge on vessels (£70 per double transit) for the raising and lowering of the lifting bridge, it being thought to be the first introduction of such a charge on the many lifting and swing bridges in the country. The Inspector heard evidence of charges (or the absence of them) at all other bridges in the country, including the Tower Bridge, and subsequently the Secretary of State directed the local authority to abandon the charge.

Another question which has arisen is whether a mooring charge is a ship due. Mooring charges are either charges made for the use of a mooring provided by the authority in a harbour, or a charge made by a harbour authority for the grant to a person of a licence to lay and maintain his own mooring in the harbour. Sometimes a charge is made, because the authority owns the bed of the harbour, but more often by virtue of a provision in the authority's enabling act. So far as the latter charge is concerned, the balance of legal opinion is that such a charge is not "in respect of any ship for entering, using, or leaving the harbour", although this definition has never been tested by legal action. Similarly it is thought that a charge made by a harbour authority for use of its own mooring being not a part of the infrastructure of the port, is not a ship due but rather a charge for ancillary services, and therefore not subject to an objection under Section 31. In this context it should however be noted that, where the fundus of the harbour is vested in and leased from the Crown Estate Commissioners, the Commissioners have undertaken to the Royal Yachting Association that harbour authorities shall not be permitted to charge more than the proportion of rent applicable to each individual mooring with a 25% uplift to cover administration and licensing charges. Thus the relevant harbours have a contractual limit imposed on them even if the Harbours Act does not provide a means of objection for boat owners.

Queen's Harbour Master

The powers of Queen's Harbour Masters in Naval Ports and dockyards are very much wider than those applying to civil/ commercial harbours. In Portsmouth Harbour, for example, the Queen's Harbour Master has introduced regulations prohibiting the use of sailboards throughout the enclosed area of Portsmouth Harbour (the ban not extending to certain areas in Spithead) in clear conflict with the principle of the general public right of navigation on all tidal waters. The wide powers of a Queen's Harbour Master make this a perfectly lawful exercise as indeed would all regulations affecting the navigation of craft unless a complainant were able to show that the imposition of such regulations was entirely unreasonable.

There are around the country a number of privately owned creeks, harbours and rivers whose owners are of course entitled to levy mooring charges where owners of craft wish to rent moorings or to lay their own moorings. As we have seen in the case of Fowley Marine (Emsworth) Limited -v- Gafford, the right to anchor in the course of the exercise of the public right of navigation does not extend to the laying of moorings. By the same token however it follows that the owner of the fundus will only be entitled to levy a charge on craft anchoring in the normal course of navigation by virtue of some statutory empowerment as a harbour authority, not by virtue of their ownership of the fundus. The right of navigation is superior to his property right, and anchoring is incidental to navigation.

Whether the private owner is an individual, a corporation, or even a body such as the Crown Estate Commissioners, the Duchy of Cornwall or the Duchy of Lancaster, does not alter the principle involved.

Nature Conservancy Council

A further recent incursion into the general public right of navigation on tidal waters appears in the Wildlife and Countryside Act 1981 which includes a provision under which byelaws may be made by the Nature Conservancy Council excluding pleasure craft from certain parts of Marine Nature Reserves at certain times of the year. Such byelaws have been introduced to restrict vessels from mooring and anchoring around Lundy and Skomer Islands and similar proposals are under consideration in the Menai Strait.

Oyster Fisheries

The Ministry of Agriculture, Fisheries and Food has powers under the Sea Fisheries Act to make orders establishing oyster (and mussel) fisheries. It is an offence to interfere with such a bed, including the placing of any apparatus prejudicial to the bed "except for the purpose of navigation or anchorage". It should be noted that the right to anchor does not include the right to drag one's anchor; in The Swift (1901) the owner of a vessel that dragged its anchor across the beds at Whitstable was successfully sued by the fishery company.

PUBLIC RIGHTS OF NAVIGATION ON NON-TIDAL WATERS

Public rights of navigation over non-tidal waters can be established by dedication, by statute, by custom (being used since time immemorial) or by prescription (uninterrupted user as of right over a period in excess of 20 years). It was originally believed that the right to navigate on non-tidal waters extended only to waters where there was commercial traffic, but the Cairngorm case shows that recreational traffic (in this case canoeing) can keep the right alive. Whether recreational use can create a new public right of navigation is debatable, being a question that has never been settled in Court.

Where there is no right to navigate, any attempt to do so will constitute a trespass and indeed in the case of Rawson -v- Peters (1972) an incursion by a canoeist into a valuable angling beat, even though it was not being fished on the day in question, was held to be an actionable trespass giving rise to damages and an injunction restraining further trespass.

On the question of "substantial interference with fishing rights" the Master of the Rolls said "It did not matter that there was no one fishing at the time. If the canoeing interfered with the right to fish minutes or hours afterwards there would be interference - the passage of canoes up and down the river must disturb the fish and interfere with the right of fishing - the rights of the angling club have been interfered with".

PARKING OF BOATS IN GARDENS

Although clearly not an exercise of the public right of navigation, it is convenient to examine the question under this chapter.

In the first draft of the Greater Manchester Bill in 1976, the Council had included a clause whereby the parking of caravans or boats in gardens attached to private dwelling houses would be prohibited. At common law a householder has the right to use his house and grounds for any normal domestic purpose without obtaining specific consent. This right, so far as the parking of boats is concerned, was defended successfully by the RYA on behalf of the boating interests before the House of Lords select committee who ordered the clause to be deleted from the Bill. It was argued that the normal planning law as to what constitutes reasonable use of the garden of a house would still apply, and that it was unnecessary to make a specific statutory prohibition.

It therefore remains a question of fact and degree in each case as to whether the parking of a boat, or the fitting-out of a bare hull, is a reasonable use of one's private land. In one recent case a householder parked two 50 ft catamaran hulls alongside his house in a prominent town centre site. In that case the hulls amounted to an obvious and unavoidable visual intrusion, and he was required to remove them after the local authority had served an enforcement notice.

In a contrasting case a householder took delivery of a 40 ft hull for fitting out, screened by the extension of his garden fence. The keel being set into a deep trench, the hull did not cause a visual intrusion. Enforcement proceedings by the local authority were opposed, and the defence had every prospect of success, until it was realised that the householder was also in breach of a restrictive covenant which affected his property. He then discontinued his operations and the local authority case was not decided.

Householders (especially those living in newer homes where such covenants are more likely) should, therefore, check their house deeds (or ask their solicitor to do so) before making long term plans for boat building or fitting-out at home.

Irrespective of the strict legal position, it is sensible to discuss plans with neighbouring occupiers who may feel themselves affected.

CHAPTER 9

MARINAS AND YACHT HARBOURS

In public harbours there are strict constraints imposed by statute and common law on the powers of the Harbour Board and the Harbour Master.

By contrast there are very few such constraints in the case of a privately owned marina or yacht harbour. For example the boatowner wishing to take a berth for his yacht will be required to enter into a contract, usually in standard form, containing General Conditions and sometimes additional Special Conditions.

The Landlord has the right to dictate what reasonable conditions he may wish to impose and the yachtsman who signs an agreement does so voluntarily. Unless he can establish that the conditions which were imposed were not drawn to his attention - and the onus of proof almost amounts to having to prove deliberate misrepresentation - he is legally bound by them.

There are a number of obvious clauses, and some which may appear onerous to the average yachtsman but the fact remains that he usually must accept them, if he wants a berth in the marina. This attitude is dictated largely by the question of supply and demand. If a yachtsman has a definite objection to some clause he may negotiate to have it removed from the conditions of contract before signature, but is unlikely to succeed unless the marina is very anxious to have his business.

Having signed, of course, he is deemed to have accepted the whole contract, conditions and all.

Over the years the RYA has been involved in attempting to obtain a set of General Conditions to be used by all marinas which are fair to both parties. By and large that work has been successful so long as marinas use the agreed TYHA and BMIF conditions which were passed by the Office of Fair Trading as not being unlawful.

The General Conditions are available from the BMIF offices at Meadlake Place, Thorpe Lea Road, Egham, Surrey,TW20 8HE.

There are, perhaps, only three points which require greater clarification from the point of view of the yachtsman.

SELLING YOUR YACHT IN A MARINA

The usual General Conditions for a private marina stipulate that "no part of the marina or yacht harbour or premises or any vessel or vehicle while situated therein or thereon shall be used by the owner for any commercial purposes".

This clause covers the possibility of anybody setting up in permanent business within the area of the privately owned marina and deals with the itinerant yacht repairer as well. It protects the marina owner also against the use of his area as a base from which to sell your yacht.

Quite often, the Special Conditions, which are entirely within the responsibility of each marina owner, go further in that they impose a further condition that if a yacht is sold whilst upon their premises a commission will be payable to the marina owner for providing a site upon which the yacht may be exhibited for sale. It has, on occasion, been contended that even if the "resident" yacht is not actually on the premises when the sale is effected, a commission would have been chargeable by the marina.

Opinions will differ about the facts in each case but it is clearly advisable, if you want to avoid liability for payment of such commission, to make certain that the yacht is not subject to a clause such as that mentioned above nor to a clause which would empower the marina to withdraw the licence to moor the yacht.

Upon a yacht sale, the new purchaser is not automatically entitled to assume that the berth which the yacht occupies will necessarily pass to him. In the majority of cases this is not so. Equally, there is a clause in the General Conditions which requires notification of the change to a new owner which could be used either to invite the new owner to continue the berthing licence, or to obtain his address for the purpose of telling him that the licence is revoked, and that he will not be offered a new one.

WORK ON THE YACHT WITHIN THE MARINA

Since many marinas maintain a work force for the repair and maintenance of yachts, their agreements will contain a general condition which prohibits anything other than minor running repairs or minor maintenance being carried out by the owner of the yacht or his agents, and will also probably stipulate exactly how and where warranty work may be carried out by suppliers. However inequitable it may seem there is nothing unlawful about the practice of demanding an access fee from visiting engineers carrying out warranty work.

Such conditions may also prohibit an owner from working on his own yacht, and the contract should be read with great care by any owner who intends to do that.

SUB-LETTING

The General Conditions stipulate that nothing "shall entitle an Owner to the exclusive use of a particular berth". The agreement aims to provide his yacht with a berth, not necessarily the same one forever.

Furthermore, unless the owner of the yacht has the prior consent of the marina operator, the owner shall not lend or transfer the berth (the licence being personal to the owner relating to the particular vessel and non-assignable) nor shall he use the berth for any other vessel.

This second clause also provides that, having given notice in writing of an absence of more than twenty eight days, the owner may qualify for some part of any proceeds of re-letting in his absence. This is the general tenor of a lengthy clause which should be read most carefully as should any Special Conditions which may add to the generality.

In practice, not many owners have a continuous absence of more than twenty eight days and the clauses effectively allow the marina owner to re-let any berth which is vacant.

Although many yachtsmen benefit from such an arrangement since they can thereby use a vacant mooring when they arrive at a marina that would be otherwise closed to visitors, most yachtsmen must also resign themselves to paying for the space on a full-time basis whether they are there or not and cannot expect any rebate unless the most stringent conditions are adhered to.

CHAPTER 10

RATING OF INDIVIDUAL MOORINGS

There are four essential ingredients for rateable occupation:-

(a) There must be actual occupation or possession.

(b) Occupation must be exclusive for the particular purposes of the possessor.

(c) Possession must be of some value or benefit to the possessor.

(d) Possession must not be for too transient a period.

Before rates can be levied on the occupation of land, it must be established that the land lies within the local authority rating area. In most cases the local authority boundary will stop at the low water mark, but in a number of places, including Brighton, Torquay, Lowestoft and Southwold, areas below the low water mark have been added by private Act of Parliament.

Similarly where a tidal creek or river lies within the area of a local authority it will be part of the jurisdiction of the authority unless the river is so wide that (in the words of the ancient test) a man cannot see what another is doing on the far bank.

In the course of the debate on the Rates Act 1984, the RYA successfully lobbied for a codification and amendment of the law affecting the rating of moorings. The result is that moorings are now exempt from rates provided they are:-

(a) Used or intended to be used by a boat or ship; and

(b) Equipped only with a buoy attached to an anchor, weight or other device

  (i) resting on or in the bed of the sea or any river or other waters when in use;

  (ii) designed to be raised from the bed from time to time.

This in effect means that all "swinging" moorings of the conventional type are exempt, whether secured by a single block, anchor or weight, or attached to a ground chain, or to a series of anchors, provided that they are designed to be raised for renewal or inspection from time to time.

Also exempt are fore-and-aft moorings of the same general design as the swinging moorings, where the yacht has a buoy at each end. Not exempt, clearly, are driven-pile and screw-pile moorings, other permanently fixed moorings and bankside moorings.

The Rates Act 1984 also enables Valuation Officers to assess individual moorings collectively so as to allow Local Authorities to serve rates demands on the authority controlling and receiving the fees for moorings. This will only apply to fixed moorings (e.g. piles, marinas, river bank moorings etc.) but will transfer to the authority controlling the harbour or other stretch of water responsibility for collecting a contribution to the total assessment from each of the mooring holders.

This method of collection should result in lower rates liabilities than would otherwise arise through individual demands. The authority responsible for the payment of rates must, if requested by the occupier of a mooring, supply information to enable the occupier to calculate his proportion of the total rate liability based on information provided by the Valuation Officer. Any occupier of a rateable mooring may apply to have his mooring separately assessed.

CHAPTER 11

TRAILING IN THE UK

Scope of this Chapter

This chapter summarises road vehicle law affecting those trailing boats or roof-racking dinghies, masts or other boat equipment.

No attempt is made to deal comprehensively with regulations applying to yachts larger than those designed to be trailed and sailed.

Further reference may be made to:-

The Road Vehicles (Construction and Use) Regulations 1986 SI 1078. The Road Vehicles Lighting Regulations 1989 SI 1796.

GENERAL DUTY TO MAKE LOADS AND PROJECTIONS SAFE

All vehicles and trailers, and their parts and accessories, must at all times be kept in such condition that no possible danger is caused to any person. The same principle applies to the weight, distribution and adjustment of any load carried on a vehicle or trailer.

Even if an overhanging mast or protruding outboard motor does not infringe any of the detailed size limitations set out below, carrying or towing it will nonetheless contravene the law if by doing so you cause a possible danger to other road users.

Fines can be imposed if this principle or any of the other regulations are breached. Anyone injured could make a civil claim against the person responsible. Trailers and their loads should therefore be carefully maintained, secured and protected. Loads on roof-racks should be secure and where necessary marked, protected and lit.

INSURANCE

The towing vehicle and the boat/trailer combination should be separately insured. Vehicle insurers should be told if it is to be used for towing.

Liability for damage caused by the boat/trailer combination when:

attached to the towing vehicle; or

after it has become accidentally detached from it ;

should be covered under the third party liability section of the vehicle policy. Damage caused to the boat/trailer would have to be claimed under the boat policy.

When the boat/trailer has been deliberately detached from the towing vehicle, any liability for damage caused by it must be claimed under the boat policy.

LENGTH RESTRICTIONS

The trailer itself

A trailer towed by an ordinary car must not be longer than 7m (excluding the hitching device) nor wider than 2.3m. If you tow with a goods vehicle weighing more than 3500kgs and your trailer has at least four wheels then the trailer may be up to 12m long.

The trailer and towing vehicle combination

The maximum permitted overall length of the trailer and tow vehicle combination is 18m (excluding projecting parts of the load). However if the trailer is constructed and normally used for carrying an 'indivisible load of exceptional length' such as a boat, then the overall length of the towing vehicle must not exceed 9.2m; and the overall length of the combination of vehicles must not exceed 25.9m including any projection of the load; if it does, you must tell the police in advance and carry an assistant with you.

Roof-rack loads

The maximum permitted length of a load carried on a single vehicle is 18.3m, which is much longer than could safely becarried on either a passenger car or small commercial vehicle.

Restrictions on roof-rack loads will therefore be governed by the rules relating to projections, detailed below.

WIDTH RESTRICTIONS

It is important to distinguish between the permitted width of the trailer itself; the extent to which a load may project on either side of the trailer; the overall width of the trailer and the load carried on it.

Trailers towed by ordinary cars should not be wider than 2.3m. If you use a towing vehicle weighing more than 3500kgs this width is increased to 2.5m.

No load should project more than 305mm sideways from the trailer, nor may the total width of the trailer and any sideways projection exceed 2.9m.

The effect of these rules is that boats up to 2.9m wide may be carried on standard trailers.

If you wish to tow a boat wider than 2.9m you must tell the police in advance. If the boat width exceeds 3.5m you must both tell the police and carry an assistant with you. The maximum permitted width of a load is 4.3m.

HEIGHT RESTRICTIONS

There is no legal maximum height for a boat trailer and its load, or for a load carried on a motor vehicle. However, the general rule requiring that loads be safely attached and distributed should be borne in mind.

The trailer manufacturing industry suggest a maximum height of 3m, or 1.7 times the wheel track of the trailer, to be good practice. Equipment should always be stored so as to keep the centre of gravity of the load as low as possible.

FRONT AND REAR OVERHANGS

Subject to certain conditions a load may extend beyond the front or rear of, or be wider than, a vehicle carrying it.

The regulations use the terms 'forward and rearward projection' and define these as being those parts of the load which extent beyond the foremost and rearmost points of the vehicle on which the load rests.

Projections may need to be marked, protected and lit.

Forward projections

If more than 2m, you must carry an assistant and fit end and side marker boards. If more than 3.05m you must also tell the police in advance. If more than 4.5m, extra side marker boards must be fitted.

Rearward projections

If the rear projection of the load exceeds 1m, it must be marked so as to be clearly visible, both to the rear and on both sides (e.g. by using a bright red or orange plastic bag or rag).

A rearward projection extending between 2m and 3.05m must be fitted with an end marker board. If it extends beyond 3.05m a rear marker board and two side marker boards are needed, the police must be told in advance and an assistant must be carried. Extra side marker boards are needed if the rearward projection exceeds 5m.

End marker boards should be triangular, with two sides of equal length. The triangle base and height must both be not less than 610mm and the board should be marked with alternate red and white stripes. Side marker boards should consist of similarly marked right angle triangular boards not less than 610mm in height and 1520mm in length. Diagrams of such boards are given in the Regulations (S.I. 1078 page 166).

Protection:

All projections should be protected so as not to be capable of causing any danger. It is particularly important to protect the exposed blades of an outboard motor mounted on a boat's transom: there have been a number of prosecutions for failure to do so.

Lighting

This is covered in the section on lighting on page 95.

WEIGHTS OF MOTOR VEHICLES AND TRAILERS

The Regulations use the following weight definitions:

axle weight	-		the sum of weights transmitted to the road surface by that axle
gross weight	-	(a)	in relation to a motor vehicle, the sum of the weight transmitted to the road surface by all the wheels of the vehicle
		(b)	in relation to a trailer, the sum of all the weights transmitted to the road surface by all the wheels of the trailer and of any weight of the trailer imposed on the drawing vehicle
maximum gross weight	-	(a)	in the case of a trailer equipped with a rating plate, the maximum gross weight shown on the plate
		(b)	in any other case, the weight which the trailer is designed or adapted not to exceed when travelling by road
kerbside weight	-	(a)	in the case of a motor vehicle, its weight when it carries no person and no load other than loose tools and equipment with which it is normally equipped and a full supply of fuel in its tank;
		(b)	in the case of a trailer, its weight when carrying no person and is otherwise unladen
laden weight gross weight	- -		in relation to a trailer, both mean the unladen (or kerbside) weight of the trailer plus any load it is carrying.

The relevant weights can be checked using a local weighbridge.

There are no prescribed minimum power/weight ratios for passenger car and trailer combinations. The weight of a goods vehicle must not exceed 1000kg for each 4.4kw of engine power. Boatowners should always bear in mind the overall requirement for the vehicle/trailer/load combination to be roadworthy.

Weight Marking

Unbraked trailers are required to be marked, in a conspicuous place on the nearside, with the maximum gross weight.

Heavy goods vehicle trailers exceeding 1020kg unladen weight must carry a plate showing the details specified in Schedule 8 to the Construction and Use Regulations.

BRAKES

All trailers must be fitted with brakes if either:-

the sum of the trailer's design axle weights exceeds 750kgs; or its laden weight exceeds its maximum gross weight; or the laden weight of the trailer exceeds half the towing vehicle's kerbside weight.

All trailers required to be fitted with brakes must also be equipped with a parking brake.

Trailers first used before 1 April 1983 may be fitted with overrun or "inertia" brakes which apply automatically if the trailer overruns. Such brakes must be efficient but no specific performance level is set.

Trailers first used from 1 April 1983 may also be fitted with overrun brakes but couplings must be damped and matched with the brake linkage. Brake design should have undergone a type approval test and braking efficiency must be at least 45%. The parking brake must be capable of holding the laden trailer on an 18% gradient. Trailers should also be fitted with an emergency device which will stop the trailer automatically if it becomes uncoupled. This does not apply to a single-axle trailer up to 1500kgs maximum gross weight if fitted with a chain or cable which will prevent the coupling head from touching the ground if it becomes uncoupled.

Heavier trailers must have brakes, and trailers in excess of 3500kgs total laden weight must have fully powered brakes operated by the braking system of the towing vehicle.

TYRES

It is illegal to mix cross ply and radial tyres on the same axle of a trailer. It is essential that tyres are suitable for the use to which they are being put, have a sufficient depth of tread and be free from any defect which might in any way cause damage either to the road surface, persons in the towing vehicle, or other persons using the road. Tyres must be correctly inflated; advice on correct inflation pressure should be obtained from the trailer manufacturer or tyre supplier. The tyres of trailers first used after April 1987 must be designed and maintained to support the trailer's maximum axle weight at its maximum permitted speed of 60mph.

Minimum tyre tread depth

The minimum legal tread depth for car and trailer tyres is 1.6mm throughout a continuous band comprising the central three quarters of the breadth of tread and round the entire circumference of the tyre.

The previous UK standard for tyres on cars, lorries, buses and motorcycles was a minimum of 1mm of tread in a continuous band across three quarters of the tread pattern with visible tread on the remaining quarter.

The new standard applies to:

- cars, meaning passenger vehicles which can carry up to 8 seated passengers in addition to the driver;
- light goods vehicles, (such as light vans) which have a maximum gross weight of up to 3500kgs;
- light trailers, which have a maximum gross weight of up to 3500kgs.

The maximum penalty for driving a vehicle with less than the legal minimum of tread depth is a fine of £1000.

SUSPENSION, BEARINGS, AND MUDGUARDS AND REGISTRATION PLATE

For those who trail long distances, it may be an advantage to have larger wheels than the manufacturer's normal specification.

Trailers bought from manufacturers can be expected to comply with the regulations. If building a trailer or renovating an old one, bear in mind that it must be fitted with suspension and mudguards. Efficient suspension is important because the road impact on a small wheel is large and it is more likely to collapse than a car wheel.

It is not advisable to attempt the home building of a trailer without very careful study of the Regulations.

If a road trailer is immersed while launching a boat, there is considerable risk of subsequent corrosion both to bearing surfaces and those parts of the trailer framework which may retain water. Corrosion is likely to be particularly severe if there is immersion in salt water; this should be avoided whenever possible. Hosing down well after immersion is essential.

The trailer registration number plate must be identical in shape, colour and characteristics to the plate on the towing vehicle. It must be illuminated at night.

LIGHTING

The 1989 Lighting Regulations introduced a number of changes which affect the lighting of boat trailers.

The following table summarises these rules.

TYPE OF TRAILER	LIGHTS REQUIRED
ALL TRAILERS, irrespective of age or size	2 rear position lamps 2 rear red stop lamps Rear white registration plate lamp(s) 2 rear red retro-reflectors (maximum of 400mm from the side of the trailer)
Trailers manufactured after 1 September 1965	2 rear amber direction indicators
Trailers manufactured after 1 April 1980	1 rear red fog lamp
Trailers manufactured after 1 October 1990	2 non-triangular white forward facing retro-reflectors
Trailers manufactured after 1 October 1990 and wider than 2.1m (note: trailer, not load width)	2 forward facing white end outline marker lamps 2 rearward facing red outline marker lamps(White and red lamps on one side of a trailer may be combined into a single lamp with a single light source)
Trailers longer than 5m (excluding hitching device and load overhang)	At least 2 (and more as required by length) amber side facing retro-reflectors on each side of trailer. (Reflectors within 1m of rear may be red)
Trailers whose gross maximum weight exceeds 3500kgs, (unless manufactured before 1 August 1982 with an unladen weight of less than 1020kgs).	Rear marking board composed of red fluorescent and yellow retro-reflecting stripes. (Note: this requirement does not apply to a trailer carrying two or more boats).

The lighting of wide or overhanging loads

Wide loads, or loads which overhang the carrying vehicle or trailer, may need to be fitted with extra lights and reflectors.

Wide trailers and wide trailer loads

Boats trailers generally need not carry white front position lamps (Schedule 1, Table VI). However:

- a trailer which projects sideways more than 400mm beyond the illuminated area of the towing vehicle's front position lamp on that side must fit fit a forward facing white lamp;
- a trailer whose load projects in a similar way must have a forward facing white lamp fitted to either the trailer or the load.

Regulation 21 specifies in detail how these lamps should be fitted.

The lighting of overhanging loads

Additional lamps and reflectors must be fitted to loads which project (forward or rearward) more than 1m beyond the carrying vehicle or the trailer.

A load projecting rearwards more than 1m (whether on a motor vehicle or trailer) must be lit by an additional rear lamp and a red retro-reflector fitted not more than 1m from the rear of the load. In practice, the need for such a lamp is usually avoided when carrying an overhanging boat on a trailer by either fitting an extension to the trailer, so that the rear lighting board is positioned vertically below the rearmost part of the load, or by fitting the lighting board to the transom of the boat. If either these methods of fitting is adopted, care should be taken that a boat mast does not overhang the aft end of the boat by more than 1m.

A lighting board should not be positioned more than 1.5m from the ground (or 2.1m 'if the structure of the vehicle makes this impracticable'). Trailers made before 1 October 1985 are permitted to have their rear lamps up to 2.1m above the ground.

A load which is carried on a motor vehicle and which projects forward more than 1m from the front of the vehicle must be lit by an additional front facing white lamp and white retro-reflector fitted not more than 1m from the front end of the load.

USING A BOAT TRAILER ON THE ROAD

Driving Licence

A vehicle towing a trailer should not be driven by the holder of a provisional licence.

Speeds

The speed limit for towing a trailer behind a passenger car is 50 mph, or 60 mph on motorways and dual carriageways.

Towing on motorways and dual carriageways

Towing is prohibited in the outside lane of a three or four lane carriageway or motorway, or at any place where all three lanes are open for use by traffic proceeding in the same direction, except when passing another vehicle of such exceptional width that it can only be passed by entering such a lane.

On a two lane carriageway or motorway, both lanes may be used.

Detached trailers

A trailer detached from the towing vehicle and left to stand on a road must have at least one wheel prevented from revolving, either by means of a brake, chain, chock or other efficient device. Failure to do so is an offence.

A detached trailer left to stand on the road between sunset and sunrise must be lit. This means that every

- rear position lamp;
- rear registration plate lamp;
- side marker lamp;
- end out-line marker lamp;

must be kept lit and unobscured. Boat trailers need not normally be fitted with front position lamps when attached to the towing vehicle, but these lamps must be fitted and lit before the trailer is left detached on a road at night.

CHAPTER 12

DOCUMENTATION FOR TRAILING ABROAD

PERSONAL

Passport

A passport is required for all overseas travel but not for journeys to the Republic of Ireland.

Helmsman's Overseas Certificate of Competence

The Certificate is recommended, particularly if venturing into European inland waterways or if taking a powered craft abroad.

In Italy a certificate should be held by all boat users and in the Netherlands by those operating speedboats capable of more than 20kph.

It is obtainable from the RYA on the recommendation of any club, sailing school or official in a sailing-related position of responsibility who can attest to the applicants competence. The Certificate is free to members, £15 to non-members. Contact the RYA for an application form.

Insurance

Personal holiday and health insurance is recommended although completion of DHSS Form E111 will often obviate the need for the latter in the European Community.

VEHICLE

A vehicle registration document should be carried.

An insurance green card should be obtained from your insurers.

Some form of vehicle breakdown and recovery insurance is advisable.

An international driving licence should be carried outside the European Community and a translation of your driving licence if visiting Italy.

TRAILER

In most European countries the overall length of vehicle and trailer must not exceed 18m; the maximum width is generally 2.5m. In Switzerland, trailers attached to light motor vehicles without four-wheel drive must not exceed 6m in length and 2.3m width.

BOAT

Boats can generally be taken temporarily from one European country to another for recreational purposes without payment of customs duty or VAT

Registration

For travel to Spain and France, registration is compulsory; inallother countries it is strongly recommended.

SMALL SHIPS REGISTER : This is an adequate alternative to full registration for the purposes of foreign travel. The fee is £10 and registration lasts five years or until a change of ownership, if earlier. Application forms can be obtained from the DVLA Swansea, SA99 1BX .

FULL REGISTRATION : Registration under Part I of the Merchant Shipping Act 1894 involves official measurement of the yacht and costs in the region of £350 for perpetual registration. Full details of the benefits of full registration, and application procedure are given in Chapter 1.

In France, very small craft are exempt from registration, the dividing line falling approximately between a Laser dinghy (which should be registered) and a Topper (which need not). The precise details of the exemption are as follows :-

Canoes, pedalos, rigid single-handed sailing craft with a beam of less than 1.15m and a metric product of length x beam x depth of less than 1.5m; other rigid craft, sail or motor, with a beam of less than 1.2m and a metric product of length x beam x depth of less than 2m; motorised inflatables less than 2.75m in length and 1.2m in beam and with an air volume of 350 litres or less; sailing inflatables less than 3.7m in length and with less than 7m square of sail area. These are referred to collectively as "engins de plage" and are not permitted to go more than 300m offshore.

Customs Documents

Although there are in theory no customs barriers between EC States, there remains the possibility that overseas customs authorities may carry out spot checks that yachts in private use belonging to non-residents (including holiday makers) to ensure that VAT has been paid. For owners with the original VAT documentation, this will not present a problem. For others, there is a presumption of VAT payment for all craft built before 31st December 1984 that were in EC territory on 31st December 1992/ 1st January 1993, and evidence of these points will ensure exemption from VAT. For owners unable to prove payment of VAT, or the necessary age of their craft, further advice should be sought from the RYA Legal Office on obtaining a VAT exemption certificate from HM Customs and Excise.

For non-EC States a carnet or customs bond is still required for owners taking their craft to the following States:-

FINLAND	-	Canoes and inflatables over 5.5m.
HUNGARY	-	All boats except kayaks or canoes under 5.5m.
MOROCCO	-	All powered craft.
ROMANIA	-	All boats except canoes and inflatables without engines under 5.5m.
TURKEY	-	All boats.

A Carnet can be obtained from the AA or RAC.

Insurance

Boat insurance against all the usual marine perils is strongly recommended. Third party insurance is compulsory in Italian waters for powered craft over 3hp and an Italian translation of the certificate or policy should be carried. This can be obtained from your broker. Third party insurance is also compulsory for boats using the Swiss lakes.

CHAPTER 13

A SUMMARY OF STATUTE LAW AFFECTING PLEASURE CRAFT

Although pleasure craft in this country are among the least regulated in the developed world, a number of Acts and Regulations do affect certain pleasure craft and pleasure craft used for certain purposes and this chapter covers the more important aspects of this body of legislation, as it relates to pleasure craft used for private purposes, chartering and teaching and to club launches and those in charge of such craft.

All Acts and Regulations mentioned below are available from HMSO, PO Box 276, London SW8 5DT, tel : 071 873 9090. Merchant Shipping Notices can be obtained from Marine Survey Offices.

PLEASURE YACHTS IN COMMERCIAL USE

The Merchant Shipping (Vessels in use for sport or pleasure) Regulations 1993 draw the distinction between yachts used for private purposes, and yachts used for commercial purposes whether for instruction, charter, the carrying of passengers, or any other similar purposes.

For yachts used privately (and that includes bona fide club owned yachts) the exemptions from most of the construction and equipment rules in the Merchant Shipping Acts remain intact. For commercially used yachts these exemptions have now largely been withdrawn unless the yacht complies with the Department of Transport's Code of Practice. This Code of Practice is intended to cover most of the points relating to merchant ships laid out elsewhere in the Merchant Shipping Acts and Regulations, but in a form that is relevant to the particular construction and circumstances of use of pleasure yachts.

PASSENGERS

Much depends upon the question of whether vessels are carrying "passengers". A passenger is defined as "any person not employed or engaged in any capacity on board on the business of the vessel (or travelling by reason of any circumstances which could not have been prevented, i.e. shipwreck) and not being children under one year of age". In a recent High Court case it was held that the term "engaged" implied the need for a binding contractual agreement, even though the person engaged may be unpaid or may even have paid the shipowner for the voyage.

Merchant Shipping (Safety Convention) Act 1949.

PLEASURE YACHTS USED ENTIRELY FOR PRIVATE PURPOSES

(i) Although registration is no longer compulsory for any British owned yacht, most owners wish to register, particularly if going overseas, and this may be on the Part 1 Register of British Shipping, or the Small Ships Register.
Merchant Shipping Acts 1894 and 1983 and Merchant Shipping (Small Ships Register) Regulations 1983/1470

(ii) Owners or masters of pleasure craft over 80 tons GRT and 24m in length and sail training ships may be subject to regulations regarding the certification of deck officers unless eligible for exemption under Section 44 of the Merchant Shipping Act 1970.
Merchant Shipping (Certification of Deck Officers) Regulations 1985/1306

(iii) Pleasure yachts in Class XII (over 13.7m) are subject to life saving and fire appliance rules.
Merchant Shipping (Life Saving and Fire Appliances) Regulations 1980-86

(iv) Pleasure craft of 20 tons GRT and above proceeding to sea are liable to an annual payment in respect of light dues, and Customs Forms C1331 are passed to Trinity House to enable them to determine what liability for light dues may have arisen.
Merchant Shipping (Mercantile Marine Fund) Act 1898

PLEASURE YACHTS LET ON CHARTER

Under Section 94 of the Public Health Acts Amendment Act 1907 (as amended) pleasure yachts let on charter may be required to be licensed. Licences are issued by the appropriate Local Authority (or, in a few special cases, under special Local Authority Acts). The present law applies throughout England and Wales by virtue of the Local Government Act 1972. The only craft requiring a licence are pleasure boats and vessels which are either :-

(a) "let for hire to the public";
(b) "used for carrying passengers for hire".

Persons in charge of navigation of craft used for carrying passengers for hire are also themselves required to be licensed (see "Boatman's Licences" below).

In the view of the RYA, pleasure yachts let on charter are serviced by "crew" rather than "passengers". They will not therefore fall to be considered for licensing under (b) above. A yacht let to a friend or on a casual basis will not be "let for hire to the public" but yachts which are regularly advertised for charter will be so let.

The letting of a private yacht (i.e. parting with possession temporarily) will require a licence only if there is a commercial element (i.e. some pecuniary reward is envisaged) and the yacht is let to the public (e.g. by advertisement rather than purely as a private arrangement). Any arrangement between a member of an unincorporated club and the club will not amount to "a letting for hire", as it falls within the definition of mutual trading.

POWERS OF DISTRICT COUNCILS TO LICENCE VESSELS

By the Local Government Act 1972 District Councils were required to operate Section 94 of the Public Health Acts Amendment Act 1907 but many District Councils have not appreciated this fact and have no licensing system. If you do require a licence the District Council may charge an appropriate fee and impose conditions. Such conditions will relate to the protection of the hirers or passengers (as the case may be) for that is the only purpose of the section. Some District Councils have attempted to impose Load Line Certification together with burdensome survey requirements and restraints on areas of operation and length of passage. These are generally outside the scope of the powers of Section 94 and may be objected to for that reason.

CLUB LAUNCHES

Club launches are affected by the Merchant Shipping Acts (1894, 1964, 1970 and 1979), the Merchant Shipping (Safety Convention) Act 1949 and the Public Health Acts Amendment Act 1907. Those who "drive" them may be required to have a DoT or other "licence" (see "Boatman's Licences" below).

It is clear from existing case law and the statutes that club launches cannot be said to be carrying only crew. Most of those on board must be described as "passengers" for they are in no way working the ship.

Survey

(a) More than twelve passengers :

Launches carrying more than twelve passengers must be surveyed (Section 271 MSA 1894 as amended by Section 17 MSA 1964). Apply for Form Survey 6 from your local Department of Trade Marine Survey office if your club is operating such a vessel. The requirements are stringent and may prohibit a petrol driven engine.

Launches carrying more than twelve passengers are subject to these regulations whether or not they are "let on hire to the public" and whether or not "passengers" have paid money. Section 94 of the Public Health Acts Amendment Act 1907 specifically exempts vessels which are already "licensed" by the Department of Transport and thus vessels with passenger certificates do not need a Local Authority licence under Section 94.

(b) Twelve or less passengers :
Club launches carrying twelve or fewer passengers will only require a Local Authority licence if they are "let on hire to the public" or are "used for carrying passengers for hire". If the service is provided free or is merely reflected in general club membership fees then the vessel will not be subject to the statute for there is no element of "hire to the public" or "carrying passengers for hire". Such vessels are not subject to DoT survey.

TEACHING ESTABLISHMENTS

The RYA takes the view, and this has been accepted by Local Authorities in England at least, that pleasure yachts used for training are not "let for hire to the public" since the payment relates to the tuition being received. Equally those on board are "crew" and such vessels cannot be said to be "carrying passengers for hire".

Hence, the RYA is of the opinion that such vessels do not fall to be licensed under Section 94 of the Public Health Acts Amendment Act 1907.

BRITISH WATERWAYS BOARD AND OTHER INLAND NAVIGATIONS

As mentioned above, Section 94 applies to pleasure boats and vessels which are "let for hire to the public" or "used for carrying passengers for hire". Section 94 has now been amended so that no licence will be required under that Section for pleasure boats and vessels whilst on any canal owned or managed by the British Waterways Board even though they are "let for hire to the public" or "carrying passengers for hire". Such vessels remain subject to the Board's own requirements as to registration, construction and use.

The Board, and the National Rivers Authority are two authorities which presently demand vessels on their water to conform with their regulations as to construction and use. No doubt in the future there will be other authorities controlling inland waterways which produce their own special construction and use regulations. In 1993 the BWB and NRA agreed a joint set of regulations to cover all waters under their control. If you are buying a vessel for use on their waterways, it is essential to ensure that it is built in compliance with these rules.

LOAD LINE REGULATIONS

The Merchant Shipping (Load Lines) Act 1967 applies to all ships except ships of war, ships solely engaged in fishing and pleasure yachts (which term has been redefined by the 1993 Pleasure Yacht Regulations).

BOATMAN'S LICENCES

Merchant Shipping Notice Number M1036 to owners and persons in charge of small passenger vessels is issued by the Department of Transport and applies to club launches.

To ensure the safe handling of such vessels which carry limited numbers of passengers and which ply in smooth or partially smooth waters or go only short distances to sea, the DoT will issue Boatman's Licences to persons suitably qualified. So far as club launches are concerned, the Notice applies to Class IV and V vessels carrying not more than 250 passengers. A candidate for a Boatman's Licence requires that an applicant must be eighteen or over, must not be suffering from any disease or disability which could make it unsafe for him to be in charge of a passenger vessel, and must pass an eyesight test and an oral test in practical seamanship and local pilotage. This test will include manoeuvring, rules of the road, use of life-saving equipment and fire fighting appliances, knowledge of fire precautions and weather reporting systems and an oral test in local pilotage (e.g. knowledge of the coastline, buoys, tidal streams etc).

Those holding Second Mate, Mate (Home Trade), Second Hand, a Class V Certificate under the Merchant Shipping (Certification of Deck Officers) Regulations 1980, DoT Yachtmaster (Coastal), or an RYA Coastal Skipper Certificate or higher will not be required to undergo these tests. Application forms can be obtained from any marine office.

The licence will be restricted to the area in which the holder has passed a test of local pilotage or produced evidence to show that he has adequate experience. Club launches may legally carry more than twelve passengers only in accordance with the limits shown on the Passenger Certificate and persons in charge of such vessels should, therefore, hold a Boatman's licence valid for the limits within which the vessel is employed.

Certain local Authorities and Harbour Authorities issue their own Boatman's Licences and require all passenger vessels plying within their areas to carry a licensed boatman. Possession of a DoT Boatman's Licence will not relieve the holder from complying with any legal requirements of such Local or Harbour Authority. Application for licences should be made to:

Department of Transport
Spring Place105 Commercial Road
Southampton SO1 0ZD
Tel: 0703 329100

LOG BOOKS

The requirement imposed by Section 68 of the Merchant Shipping Act 1970 that an official logbook shall be kept in every ship registered in the United Kingdom does not apply to:

(a) a ship belonging to a general lighthouse authority;
(b) a ship of less than 25 gross tons; or
(c) a privately used pleasure yacht.

Merchant Shipping (Official Log Books) Regulations 1981/569

CLASSIFICATION OF SHIPS

For the purposes of the Merchant Shipping Acts, all ships are classified. Club launches are likely to be considered under Class IV or V. Privately used pleasure yachts over 13.7 metres (45ft) LOA are normally classed under Class XII. The full classification is as follows:

Class I	Passenger ships engaged on voyages (not being short international voyages) any of which are long international voyages.
Class II	Passenger ships engaged on voyages (not being long international voyages) any of which are short international voyages.
Class II (A)	Passenger ships engaged on voyages of any kind other than international voyages.
Class III	Passenger ships engaged only on voyages in the course of which they are at no time more than 70 miles by sea from their point of departure and not more than 18 miles from the coast of the United Kingdom, and which are at sea only in fine weather and during restricted periods.
Class IV	Passenger ships engaged only on voyages in partially smooth waters, or in smooth and partially smooth waters.
Class V	Passenger ships engaged only on voyages in smooth waters.
Class VI	Passenger ships engaged only on voyages with not more than 250 passengers on board, to sea, in smooth or partially smooth waters, in all cases in fine weather and during restricted periods in the course of which the ships are at no time more than 15 miles, exclusive of any smooth waters, from their point of departure nor more than 3 miles from land.
Class VI(A)	Passenger ships carrying not more than 50 passengers for a distance of not more than 6 miles on voyages to or from isolated communities on the

islands or coast of Scotland, and which do not proceed for a distance or more than 3 miles from land.

Ships other than passenger ships :

Class VII	Ships (other than ships of Classes I, VII (A), VII (T), X, XI, and XII) engaged on voyages any of which are long international voyages.
Class VII(A)	Ships engaged in the whaling industry or employed as fish processing or canning factory ships, and ships engaged in the carriage of persons employed in the whaling, fish processing or canning industries.
Class VII(T)	Tankers engaged on voyages any of which are long international voyages.
Class VIII	Ships (other than ships of Classes II, VIII (T), IX, X, XI and XII) and other ships engaged only on voyages which are not international voyages.
Class VIII(A)	Ships other than ships of Classes II(A) to VI(A) inclusive, VIII(A) (T), IX, IX(A), X, XI and XII) and other ships engaged only on voyages which are not international voyages.
Class VIII(A)	Tankers engaged only on voyages which are not (T)international voyages.
Class IX	Tugs and tenders (other than ships of Class II, II(A), III, VI and VI(A)) which proceed to sea but are not engaged on long international voyages.
Class IX(A)	Ships (other than ships of Classes IV to VI inclusive) which do not proceed to sea.
Class IX(A)	Tankers which do not proceed to sea.
Class X	Fishing vessels other than ships of Classes I to VI (A) inclusive.
Class XI	Sailing ships (other than fishing boats and ships of Class XII) which proceed to sea.
Class XII	Privately used pleasure craft (other than ships of Classes I to VI(A) inclusive) of 45 feet in length or over.

CHAPTER 14

REPORTING TO CUSTOMS ON DEPARTURE AND ARRIVAL

For a craft voyaging between EC ports, there are no departure or arrival reporting requirements. However any pleasure craft sailing into or out of the United Kingdom from or to places abroad outside the EC territory are subject to the Pleasure Craft (Arrival and Report) Regulations 1979, made under sections 35 (4) and 42 (1) of the Customs and Excise Management Act 1979, and the Commissioners, directions also made under that Act.

A pleasure craft in the Regulations is defined as one which at the time of its arrival from abroad is being used for private recreational purposes with not more than twelve persons aboard; or any other vessel which an officer allows so to be treated for the purposes of these regulations.

Yachtsmen intending to depart from the U.K. are required to notify H. M. Customs and Excise on Form C1331, a three-part carbon-interleaved form, Part I of which constitutes notice of departure, Part II of which will be the declaration of goods on re-entry, and Part III of which will remain with the ships papers.

Duty free stores may be shipped on any registered craft (including those registered on the Small Ships Register) and on smaller craft if they are going beyond Near European Waters (i.e. Elbe to Brest) on prior application.

Recreational craft arriving back from abroad should fly a yellow flag (the "Q" flag in the International Code of Signals), from entry within the 12 mile limit until all customs formalities have been completed. The skipper or his representative must notify the arrival to a customs officer either in person or by telephone within two hours of arrival.

The report procedure applies to craft arriving from a non-EC point of departure, or where duty and/or VAT is payable on the vessel or if the vessel:-

(a) has on board any prohibited or restricted goods; or
(b) has on board live animals or birds, including domestic pets, or any other goods the importation of which is subject to any prohibition or restriction; or
(c) has on board any person who is not patrial or if patrial is not carrying a valid British passport (except in the case of arrivals from the Channel Islands or Republic of Ireland); or

(d) has any death or notifiable illness or sickness on board.

The full report procedure requires that the person responsible has fully completed Parts II and III of Form C1331 for delivery to the customs officer when he boards the vessel.

CHAPTER 15

CHARTERING

Although experience has taught a number of entrepreneurs in this country recently that yacht charter is not always a lucrative business, particularly if a commercial return on capital is desired, nonetheless a large number of yacht owners enter into short term occasional charter arrangements merely in order to subsidise some of the cost of their sailing.

Owners intending to charter their yachts would be well advised to enter into a contract with intended charterers in the form laid out at Appendix 4, further copies of which are available from the RYA. This standard form agreement is sufficiently detailed to deal with most potential points of conflict and argument arising out of the owner/charterer relationship and should be followed as closely as possible.

It will also be necessary, in most cases, to inform your insurance broker of the proposed arrangement since a considerable additional premium is often required by underwriters to cover a vessel while on charter and this must be taken into account when negotiating the charter fee.

You should also note that, if you are, as the owner of the yacht, entitled to wear a privileged ensign, this privilege does not extend to the yacht while under charter unless the charterer happens to be a member of the same club and is in possession of a warrant.

Overseas chartering is likely to become very much more widespread, following the harmonisation of VAT structures within the European Community in 1993. While the profitable part of the U.K. charter season is little more than four months, it is not unusual for bareboat charter yachts in the Mediterranean to be available for up to nine months, with an average occupancy of one hundred and twenty days. Under the terms of the Geneva Convention on the Temporary Importation of Means of Transport, the owner of a yacht may import it temporarily to any other country signatory to the convention, on a VAT free and tax free basis, but commercial use of the yacht enjoying tax-free temporary importation is not permitted. The removal of VAT differentials and harmonisation of VAT payments will have the effect of opening all the European, and particularly the Mediterranean, borders to overseas competition.

Following the introduction of the 1993 Pleasure Yacht Regulations, all chartered craft under the British flag are required to comply with a comprehensive Code of Practice covering most areas of construction, equipment, and operating limits. Owners intending to charter (except for racing purposes only) should check most carefully that their craft will comply with the Code of Practice and will probably have to invest heavily in new equipment to ensure compliance.

CHAPTER 16

INTERNATIONAL SHIPPING CONVENTIONS

In order to understand the thinking behind overseas statutory requirements, and indeed to make sense of a number of the provisions of our own Merchant Shipping Acts, it is helpful to have a knowledge of the main aspects of the international law of the sea as comprised in a number of international shipping conventions.

The most important forum for the conception and enactment of conventions is the International Maritime Organisation, based in London, which offers membership to every seafaring state in the world, and on whose committees sit a wide range of permanent delegates and experts dealing not only with new conventions but also continuously monitoring existing conventions and dealing with inter-state disputes.

So far as all yachtsmen are concerned, the one convention that has an immediate and all embracing influence from the moment of casting-off is Annex B to the Final Act of the International Conference on Safety of Life at Sea, 1960. Better known as the International Regulations for Preventing Collisions at Sea, these rules are in effect a codification of centuries of maritime practice between seamen to keep ships clear of each other. These rules, which are the foundation of those now in force, were established by custom and formed part of the general maritime law administered by the Admiralty Court in England. In 1840 Trinity House published regulations setting out recognised rules based on existing practice, but it was not until the Brussels Regulations of 1910 were agreed that an internationally recognised code came into force which itself formed the basis for the 1960 code, and which itself was updated by the IMO Conference of 1972. The regulations, which are laid out and annotated in full in RYA Booklet G2, are imported into English Law, with criminal sanctions, by Section 418 of the Merchant Shipping Act 1984.

Of particular concern to yachtsmen cruising abroad is the 1958 Geneva Convention on Territorial Sea and Contiguous Zone and the 1958 Geneva Convention on the High Seas. The first of these conventions provides the basis for the sovereignty of a state to extend beyond its land territory to a belt of sea adjacent to its coast. This is the territorial sea and is measured from the low-water line. Deeply embayed areas are included in territorial seas, unless they would cut into the territorial sea of another state. The convention provides that ships of all states, whether coastal or not, shall enjoy the right of innocent passage through the territorial sea of another state. Passage is defined as navigation either for the purpose of traversing that sea without entering internal waters, or of making for the high seas from internal waters. Passage includes stopping and anchoring, but only if incidental to ordinary navigation.

The "contiguous zone" is defined as the band of water beyond the territorial sea, out to a maximum of twelve miles, up to which the coastal state may exercise the controls necessary to prevent infringements of its customs, fiscal, immigration or sanitary regulations within its territory or territorial sea. The convention also provides that coastal states may only extend their criminal jurisdiction to foreign ships passing through their territorial waters, either to investigate or arrest any person, in the following cases :-

(a) If the consequences of the crime extend to the coastal state;
(b) If the crime would disturb the peace of the country or the good order of the territorial sea;
(c) If the captain of the ship or the consul of the flag country has requested assistance;
(d) If it is necessary for the suppression of illicit traffic in narcotic drugs.

The 1958 Geneva Convention on the High Seas codifies the international custom relating to freedom of navigation on the high seas. The convention provides that every state, whether coastal or not, has the right to sail ships under its flag on the high seas, and that each state shall fix the conditions for the grant of nationality to its ships, for the registration of ships in its territory, and for the right to fly its flag. Ships have the nationality of the State whose flag they are entitled to fly. There must exist a genuine link between the State and the ship; in particular, the State must effectively exercise its jurisdiction and control in administrative, technical and social matters over ships flying its flag. Each State shall issue documents to that effect to ships to which it has granted the right to fly its flag.

The Convention also provides that a ship may sail under the flag of one State only, and may not change its flag during a voyage, or while in a port of call, except in the case of a real transfer of ownership or change of registry. A ship which sails under two or more flags, according to convenience, may not claim any of the nationalities in question with respect to any other state and may be assimilated to a ship without nationality.

The Convention provides that every state shall take such measures for ships under its flag as are necessary to ensure safety at sea with regard, inter alia, to :-

(a) the use of signals, maintenance of communications, and prevention of collisions;
(b) manning and labour agreements where appropriate;
(c) the construction, equipment and seaworthiness of ships.

In the event of a collision or other incident concerning a ship in the high seas, involving the flag state's penal code, penal proceedings may only be brought in the flag state or in the master's or other officer's state of nationality.

The Convention also provides that every state shall require the master of a ship to render assistance to any person or vessel in danger, in so far as he can do without danger to his own ship or crew.

The 1956 Geneva Customs Convention on the temporary importation for private use of Aircraft and Pleasure Boats is of particular significance to cruising yachtsmen. The effect of the convention (to which Austria, Belgium, West Germany, France, Hungary, Italy, Luxembourg, Netherlands, Sweden, Switzerland and the United Kingdom were the initial signatories) is to enable cruising yachtsmen to enter foreign waters without immediately becoming liable for import duty and V.A.T. on the full value of their yachts. The convention provides that each of the contracting countries shall grant tax-free temporary importation, subject to re-exportation, and to a number of other conditions, to aircraft and boats owned by persons normally resident outside its territory. The introduction of the single EC fiscal area in 1993 reduced the importance of this Convention, but it is still of effect in non-EC Convention States.

Use of such aircraft and boats is limited to the owner and other persons normally resident outside the host country's territory. This use by other persons is normally subject to the proviso that no commercial use is made of the boat (i.e. the owner may lend it, but not charter it out while it is in the host country) although a number of countries do not enforce this particular provision.

APPENDIX I

AGREEMENT FOR CONSTRUCTION OF A NEW CRAFT

DATE OF AGREEMENT 19
PARTIES (Insert full names and address)
1. "The Builders" :
   of
2. "The Purchaser" :
   of
These terms include successors in title
PRICE * £ , payable as follows :
(a) Upon the signing of this agreement £
(b) Upon the hull being available at the Builders' premises, fully moulded, planked, plated or formed £
(c) Upon substantial completion of the fitting of the interior joinery work, installation of the engine or stepping of the mast, whichever is the earlier £
(d) Upon completion of an acceptance trial, and the signing of the satisfaction note by the Purchaser or his agent (see clause 7) £

* N.B.
(i) VAT. Where VAT is payable, it forms part of the price. The figures on this page must therefore include VAT at the rate applicable at the date of the agreement. The Government has power to alter VAT rates and classifications : any such alterations would bind both parties and be reflected in instalment payments under this agreement.
(ii) Instalments. It is suggested that instalment (a) above should normally be not more than 20% of the total price, except that it should be not more than 30% in cases where the Builders are buying in the hull or ordering the engines at an early stage. It is also suggested that instalment (d) should be not less than 10% of the total price.

These figures are no more than a guide and may be varied by agreement between the parties.

DELIVERY (see Clause 4)
Expected Date : 19
Place :
ACCEPTANCE TRIAL (see Clause 7.1)
Maximum duration : hours
Place :

AGREEMENT : The Builders will build and the Purchaser will buy a craft, subject to the within-written terms of this agreement.
SIGNED by the Builders
in the presence of :-
(Witness)
SIGNED by the Purchaser
in the presence of :-
(Witness)
SATISFACTION NOTE
(For signature after acceptance trial - see Clause 7.3)
I, the undersigned, hereby certify that the construction of the craft and the acceptance trial have been completed to my reasonable satisfaction.

This satisfaction note will not affect my statutory rights should the craft or its equipment later prove to be defective (see clause 8).
Dated : 19
SIGNED :
Signature of Purchaser or his agent

TERMS OF AGREEMENT

Specification

1. The Builders will build and the Purchaser will buy the craft ("the craft") described in the specification and drawings ("the specification") annexed to this agreement. The Builders will construct the craft in compliance with the specification. The Purchaser and/or his authorised agent shall have the right to reject all workmanship, materials and/or equipment which is not in compliance with the requirements set out in the specification. Such rejection shall be ineffective unless confirmed promptly to the Builders in writing in accordance with clause 15.

Modifications or additions

2. Any modification or additions to the specification shall not form part of this agreement until confirmed by both parties in writing.

Price and instalments

3.1 The price of the craft, and the stages at which it shall be paid by the Purchaser to the Builders, shall be as stated at the commencement of this agreement.

Price variation clause (see note 7)

3.2 If so required by the Builders, the price stated shall be increased by the addition thereto of such percentage of each instalment (other than the first) as is equal to the percentage increase in the figure at which the Index of Retail Prices stands at the date upon which the instalment falls due over the figure at which the Index stood at the date of this agreement. Further, the Builders may require the Purchaser to pay any increased costs resulting from a change in law or regulation occurring or announced between the date of this agreement and the final instalment falling due. However :

(a) no account shall be taken of increases in the price which would not have been chargeable but for the failure of the Builders to proceed with the construction of the craft with reasonable despatch;

(b) if there is a material change in the basis of compiling the Index of Retail Prices published by the Department of Employment (or by any government department upon which duties in connection with the Index shall have devolved) or if that Index is discontinued, price adjustments shall be based on some other index to be agreed from time to time by the BMIF and the RYA;

(c) to the extent that the Builders do not make an increase when demanding an earlier instalment, the entire amount of the increase shall be payable with the final instalment.

Delivery date and place

4.1 The Builders shall deliver the craft, completed in compliance with the specification, to the Purchaser or his agent by the date and at the place stated in this agreement, but subject to prior signature of the satisfaction note herein. This delivery date shall be deferred if completion is delayed due to modifications or additions to the specification or any cause whatsoever (including delay by suppliers in delivering equipment) outside the control of the Builders.

4.2 If all or any of the materials or equipment built in to the craft or appropriated to this agreement shall be seriously damaged by any cause whatever, the delivery date stated herein shall be deferred for such time as is necessary for the Builders to reinstate the work and to purchase and obtain delivery of materials or equipment in substitution for those damaged.

AGREED DAMAGES CLAUSE

This clause may be added to the printed form of agreement for construction of a new craft if it is of great importance to the Purchaser that the craft should be delivered by the date specified.

The figure to be inserted in the blank space should not be in the nature of a penalty, and may be subject to an agreed maximum. It should be a genuine pre-estimate of the loss likely to be caused to the Purchaser by the delay. The figure might well be based on the cost of chartering a comparable craft.

AGREED DAMAGES CLAUSE

If due to the Builders' failure without reasonable cause to proceed with reasonable despatch, the craft is not completed by the date set out above (as deferred under sub-clause 4.2 where necessary) and if the Purchaser has not exercised his rights under clause 5, the Builders shall pay the Purchaser * £......... in respect of each week or part of a week until the craft is completed as agreed damages for his loss of use of the craft.

Insert initials of both parties

....

....

Builders' failure to proceed

5. If the Builders fail without reasonable cause to proceed with the construction of the craft with reasonable despatch, the Purchaser shall be at liberty to remove the craft and such materials and equipment as have been purchased or appropriated by the Builders for construction of the craft, provided that payments made or tendered by the Purchaser to the Builders are at least equivalent to the cost to the Builders of the goods to be removed (including the Builders' current profit margins). If the craft is at such stage of construction that it is impracticable to remove it, the Purchaser shall be entitled to employ alternative labour and materials to proceed with the construction of the craft (and to exercise all necessary rights of access to the Builders' premises during their normal business hours), but only as far as is necessary to enable the craft to be removed. Such rights shall be without prejudice to any other rights that the Purchaser may have.

Access to craft and Builders' premises

6. Subject to the prior consent of the Builders, the Purchaser and/or his authorised agent shall have free and reasonable access to the craft and to the materials and equipment to be used in the craft, for the purpose of inspection at any time during the normal business hours of the Builders' establishment. Such consent shall not be unreasonably withheld but may be granted on terms that the Purchaser or his agent is accompanied by a representative of the Builders. Such right of access shall extend only to those parts of the Builders' premises necessary for the purpose of such inspection. If the Purchaser or his agent shall for that or any other purpose use any part of the Builders' premises and/or facilities, and whether by invitation or otherwise, he shall do

so at his own risk, unless any injury or damage to person or property is caused by or results from the negligence or any deliberate act of the Builders or of those for whom they are responsible.

Acceptance trial

7.1 Not less than twenty eight days in advance (unless a shorter time be agreed by the parties), the Builders shall notify the Purchaser in writing that the craft will be ready for an acceptance trial on a stated date. The Purchaser or his authorised agent shall present himself within seven days after that date, at an agreed time, to accompany the Builders or their representative upon an acceptance trial lasting not more than the duration stated in this agreement (such acceptance trial to be at the Builders' expense). If the Purchaser or his authorised agent shall fail to so present himself, then at the end of such seven day period, the acceptance trial shall be deemed to have taken place.

7.2 If at the end of such acceptance trial the Purchaser or his agent shall for good cause refuse to accept the craft until faults have been rectified, then the Builders shall rectify the same, and if necessary a second trial shall be held in accordance with the provisions of sub-clause 7.1.

7.3 At the satisfactory conclusion of the acceptance trial or, as the case may be, after satisfactory rectification of any faults, the Purchaser or his agent shall sign the satisfaction note contained in this agreement. The final instalment shall become payable immediately upon signature of such note or upon unreasonable failure or refusal to sign. If the Purchaser or his agent shall fail to present himself within the seven days period mentioned in sub-clause 7.1., the final instalment shall become payable at the end of such period.

7.4 If the Purchaser shall fail to take delivery of the craft within twenty eight days of the final instalment falling due, the Builders may thereafter require him to pay reasonable mooring or storage charges until he does so.

Statutory rights of Purchaser (see note 8)

8. The craft and all materials and equipment are supplied with the benefit of the undertakings (particularly as to conformity of goods with description or sample, and as to their quality or fitness for a particular purpose) which are implied by the Sale of Goods Act 1979. Nothing in this agreement shall affect those statutory rights.

Insurance (see note 9)

9. The craft and all materials and equipment supplied or installed by the Builders which are from time to time intended for the craft and within the premises of the Builders shall be insured by them. Such insurance shall be at Lloyds or with an insurance company belonging to the British Insurance Association, against all Builders' Risks in accordance with "Institute Clauses for Builders' Risks amended for Yacht and Motor Boat" until delivery. In the event of the craft, equipment or materials sustaining damage at any time before delivery, any monies received in respect of the insurance shall be applied by the Builders in making good the damage during ordinary working hours in a reasonable and workmanlike manner. However, if the Builders cannot reasonably be expected to make good such damage, then unless this agreement is determined under sub-clause 10.1 or 10.2 they shall pay to the Purchaser the monies so received (but not so as to exceed the instalments then paid by the Purchaser). The Purchaser shall not on account of the said damage or repair be entitled to reject or to make any objection to the craft, equipment or materials, or to make any claim in respect of any resultant depreciation in its or their value or utility.
The insurance liability of the Builders under this clause shall cease upon delivery of the craft to the Purchaser.

Termination of agreement in event of damage

10.1 Notwithstanding the foregoing, the Builders may in their discretion elect either to fulfil or to determine this agreement if from any cause (other than the negligence or any deliberate act of the Builders or of those for whom they are responsible) and at any time:
(a) the craft shall become a total loss or be deemed to be a constructive, arranged or compromised total loss, or
(b) the Builders' premises, plant, machinery, equipment or any of them shall be seriously damaged so as to make it impracticable for the Builders to complete the craft.
If the Builders shall elect to determine this agreement, they shall forthwith refund to the Purchaser any instalments of the purchase price received by them. This agreement will thereupon be determined in all respects as if it had been duly completed and the Purchaser shall have no further right to claim on the Builders.

10.2 If by reason of serious damage to the Builders' premises, plant or machinery, or to the craft, its equipment or the materials intended for it, the craft cannot be delivered within a reasonable time after the delivery date stated herein (as deferred under sub-clause 4.2 where necessary), the Purchaser may determine this agreement. The Builders shall thereupon refund to the Purchaser any instalments of the purchase price received by them and thereupon this agreement will be determined in all respects and neither party shall have any further right to claim on the other.

Passing of property in craft etc.

11. The craft and/or all materials and equipment purchased or appropriated from time to time by the Builders specifically for its construction (whether in their premises, water or elsewhere) shall become the property of the Purchaser upon the payment of the first instalment under this agreement or (if it be later) upon the date of the said purchase or appropriation. The Builders shall, however, have a lien upon the craft, materials and equipment for recovery of all sums due (whether invoiced or not) under the terms of this agreement or any variation or modification thereof. Any materials or equipment rejected by the Purchaser shall forthwith re-vest in the Builders.

Unpaid instalments

12. If any instalment shall remain unpaid for twenty eight days after notice has been given to the Purchaser by registered or recorded delivery post, the Builders shall be entitled to interest at 3% above the Bank of England's base rate for the time being (calculated from the date when the Builders first issued an invoice or other written request for payment of the instalment). After a further period of twenty eight days the Builders shall be at liberty to sell the craft as it then lies, or may complete and sell the craft after completion. On such re-sale the Purchaser shall be refunded any instalments previously paid, subject to deduction therefrom of any loss suffered by the Builders on the re-sale.

Copyright etc.

13. Any copyright or similar protection in all drawings, specifications and plans prepared by the Builders or their architects shall remain the property of the Builders.

Bankruptcy etc. of Purchaser

14. The Builders shall have the right to terminate this agreement by notice in writing in the event of the Purchaser becoming bankrupt or entering into any composition or arrangement with his creditors or if, being a company, it shall enter into liquidation (otherwise than for the purpose of amalgamation

or reconstruction) or any arrangement with its creditors, or shall have a receiver appointed of the whole or any part of its property.

Notices

15. Subject to clause 12, notices may be given by being handed to the addressee or sent by first class post, telex, cable or telegram to his address as shown in this Agreement (unless the addressee has by written notice to the other party substituted a different address in England as the notice address). Any notice posted shall be deemed to have been received 48 hours after the time of posting and any notice given in any other manner shall be deemed to have been received at the time when in the ordinary course it may be expected to have been received. In proving service of any notice it shall be sufficient to prove that delivery was made or that the envelope containing the notice was properly addressed and posted or that the telex, cable or telegram was properly addressed and sent (as the case may be).

Arbitration

16. All disputes arising out of or in connection with this agreement shall be submitted to a single arbitrator to be appointed, in default of agreement, by the President of the SBBNF and the Chairman of the Council of the RYA and the provisions of the Arbitration Acts 1950 to 1979 shall apply.

Miscellaneous

17.1 This agreement shall be construed according to and governed by the law of England.

17.2 The construction of this agreement is not to be affected by any marginal note.

17.3 Subject always to the statutory rights of the Purchaser, this agreement forms the entire agreement between the parties and, unless specifically agreed in writing by the Builders, no warranty, condition, description or representation is given or to be implied by anything said or written in the negotiations between the parties or their representatives prior to this agreement.

17.4 Reference to any statutory provision includes a reference to that provision as amended, extended or re-enacted and to any statutory replacement thereof (either before or after the date of this agreement).

Additional terms

18. This agreement is subject also to the special terms (if any) set out below, or attached to this agreement and signed by both parties.

NOTES

These are explanatory notes only and, although very important, do not form part of the agreement itself.

1. This form is published by the British Marine Industries Federation (BMIF) and approved by the Royal Yachting Association (RYA) and is available from both organisations.
2. It is a simple form of agreement and cannot be expected to cater for every unforeseen circumstance arising between the parties. It does attempt to define the intentions of the parties and is considered by the RYA and the BMIF to hold a reasonable balance between the purchaser and the builders.
3. It should be completed in duplicate, taking care to insert the appropriate details. Any specification, drawing, or additional clause which cannot be accommodated should be firmly attached to the agreement and signed by both parties. Additional clauses should be initialled by both parties.
4. Both parties should sign in the presence of a witness.
5. The satisfaction note must be signed by the purchaser or his agent on delivery of the completed craft.
6. If it is of great importance to the purchaser that the craft should be delivered by the date specified, a suitable "agreed damages clause" for attachment to the agreement is available from the BMIF and RYA.
7. (a) Clause 3.2 is a price variation clause which allows the builders to adjust the price to reflect inflation occurring between the dates of the agreement and the final instalment falling due. The clause should be deleted where the parties agree on a "fixed-price contract", (usually where the period between signing and final payment is likely to be short).

   (b) Builders are reminded that the clause does not permit a price increase to reflect inflation occurring between original quotation and signature of the agreement. For this reason builders should express their quotations as valid for a limited period and, if necessary, should revise them where the agreement is signed after that period.

   (c) The clause allows builders to increase the price so as to reflect all increases in the Retail Prices Index occurring after the date of the agreement. If they intend to rely on the clause, builders should base the price on current costs without the addition of any inflation factor.

8. If any defect should be discovered in the craft or its equipment after the purchaser has taken delivery, it will be in his own interests to give immediate written notice to the builders in accordance with clause 15. If a builder is to be legally liable to rectify the defect, it must usually be shown that the defect arises from a breach of this agreement or of the undertakings implied at the time of the sale by the Sale of Goods Act 1979 as amended.
   This note does not affect the purchaser's statutory rights.
9. If the purchaser leaves or arranges for others to leave any items on the builders' premises or on the craft, he should insure the item himself unless the builders expressly agree in writing to do so. However, builders should have adequate insurance cover against claims arising from their negligence which result in damage to any property on their premises.
10. Copies of this agreement may be obtained from

British Marine Industries Federation
Meadlake Place
Thorpe Lea Road
Egham
Surrey
TW20 8HE

or

The Royal Yachting Association
RYA House
Romsey Road
Eastleigh
Hampshire
S05 4YA

APPENDIX 2

MAIN HEADINGS OF ESTIMATE OF COST SCHEDULE

Summary

Section	Item	Labour £	Material £	Total £
A	Framing			
B	Planking			
C	Inside Framing			
D	Painting			
E	Deck Framing			
F	Cabin and Cockpit			
G	Steering Gear			
H	General Hull Fittings			
I	Machinery			
J	Canvas Gear			
K	Sailing Tackle			
L	Launching and Slipping			
M	Sheathing			
N	Trials			
O	Delivery			
P	Electrical Work			
Q	Dinghy			
R	Foremen's Supervision & Sawmill's Labour (Unless included in overheads)			
S	Outfit.			
T	Insurance			
U	Sundries			

Total - £

TOTALS EXTRAS

£

Overheads ______________________

Materials ______________________

Cost ______________________

Profit ______________________

TENDER PRICE

APPENDIX 3

AGREEMENT FOR THE SALE OF A SECONDHAND YACHT

An agreement prepared by the Royal Yachting Association for the sale of a secondhand yacht between persons not normally engaged in the business of selling yachts.

AN AGREEMENT made the day of 19
BETWEEN :

1. "The Vendor" :
   of
2. "The Purchaser" :
   of

The terms "Vendor" and "Purchaser" include their respective successors in title and the Vendor and Purchaser shall hereinafter be collectively referred to as "the Parties".
"The Purchase Price" : £ sterling
"The Deposit" : 10% of the Purchase Price
In respect of the sale of a [REGISTERED/UNREGISTERED] PLEASURE CRAFT
Name :
Description :
Official No. :
Port of Registry where applicable :
Now lying at :
Including all equipment, machinery and gear on board ("the Yacht") and any specific inventory attached hereto initialled by the Parties and forming part of this Agreement.

Agreement for sale

1. The Vendor hereby agrees to sell and the Purchaser agrees to purchase the Yacht free from any encumbrances (subject to the conditions and terms of this agreement), together with all her outfit gear and equipment as set out in a schedule hereto but not including stores or the Vendor's personal effects, for the Purchase Price.

Payment of deposit

2. On the signing of this agreement the Deposit is to be paid to the Vendor and the balance of the Purchase Price together with any Value Added Tax shall be payable in accordance with Clause 6.

Value Added tax

3.1 The Vendor [is/is not] a registered person for the purpose of the regulations relating to Value Added Tax and the Purchase Price [is/is not] exclusive of Value Added Tax.

Import dues and local taxes (craft lying overseas)

3.2 The Vendor warrants that the craft has been properly [temporarily/ permanently] imported into [ ] and that all appropriate local taxes and dues have been paid and that the proposed sale is in accordance with all relevant local laws and regulations.

Inspection survey

4. The Purchaser may, at a venue to be agreed at his own cost, haul out or place ashore and/or open up the Yacht and her machinery for the purposes of inspection and/or survey which, including any written report, shall be completed within [ ] days of the signing of this agreement. If any inspection requires more than superficial non-destructive dismantling the consent of the Vendor must be obtained before such work commences.

Notice of defects

5.1 Within fourteen days after completion of such inspection and/ or survey if any material defect(s) in the Yacht or her machinery other than disclosed to the Purchaser in writing prior to the signing of this agreement or any material deficiencies in her inventory, if any, shall have been found the Purchaser may either :

5.1.1 give notice to the Vendor of his rejection of the Yacht provided that the notice shall specify any material defect(s) or deficiencies; or

5.1.2 give notice to the Vendor specifying any material defect(s) or deficiencies and requiring the Vendor forthwith either to make good the same or make a sufficient reduction in the Purchase Price to enable the Purchaser to make good the same. All agreed items of work to be completed without undue delay in all circumstances and to be carried out so as to satisfy the expressly specified requirements of the Purchaser's surveyor in respect only of material defects mentioned in his report and specified in the notice to the Vendor.

5.2 If the Purchaser shall have served a notice of rejection under Clause 5.1.1, then this agreement shall be deemed to be rescinded forthwith and the Vendor shall refund to the purchaser the Deposit in accordance with Clause 8.

5.3 If the Purchaser shall have served a notice under Clause 5.1.2 requiring the Vendor to make good material defects or deficiencies or to make a reduction in the Purchase Price, and the Vendor shall not have agreed within twenty one days after the service of the notice to make good such defects or the Parties have not agreed in the twenty one days after the service of notice upon the reduction in the Purchase Price, then this agreement shall be deemed to have been rescinded on the twenty second day after the service of notice and the Vendor shall refund to the Purchaser the Deposit in accordance with Clause 8.

In the case of any deficiencies in the Yacht's inventory (if any) remaining or arising within seven days of acceptance in accordance with Clause 6 the deficiencies shall be made good or a reduction in the Purchase Price shall be agreed, failing which this agreement shall be rescinded at the option of the Purchaser only.

Acceptance of yacht

6.1 The Yacht shall be deemed to have been accepted by the Purchaser and the balance of the Purchase Price and any Value Added Tax thereon shall become due and payable in accordance with Clause 7 upon the happening of any of the following events :

6.2 The expiry of fourteen days from the date of this agreement or such extended period as may be agreed between the Parties provided that no inspection or survey has been commenced;

6.3 The expiry of fifteen days from the completion of the survey, provided that the Purchaser has not served notice under Clause 5.1;

6.4 Notification in writing by the Vendor to the Purchaser of completion of the remedial works specified in a notice given by the Purchaser under Clause 5.1.2;

Completion

7.1 Upon acceptance of the Yacht by the Purchaser, of Sale the Deposit shall be treated as part payment of the Purchase Price. Within seven days of acceptance the Purchaser shall pay the balance of the Purchase Price and any Value Added Tax thereon and the Vendor shall :

7.1.1 In the case of a **registered yacht** provide the Purchaser with the Certificate of Registry, correct and updated, together with any other documents appertaining to the Yacht and shall execute a Bill of Sale, in the prescribed form, in favour of the

Purchaser or his nominee, showing the Yacht to be free from encumbrances and completed so as to ensure transfer on the Register;
OR

7.1.2 In the case of an **unregistered yacht** (including a yacht registered on the SSR)

(a) Provide the Purchaser with a Bill of Sale in favour of the Purchaser or his nominee, together with any other documents appertaining to the Yacht;

(b) Deliver to the Purchaser any necessary delivery order or other authority enabling the Purchaser to take immediate possession of the Yacht.

7.2 Where payment is made by cheque, draft, letter of credit or other instrument, the terms of this agreement shall not be deemed to have been fulfilled until such payment is cleared into the payee's account.

Vendor's right to assign title

7.3 By delivery of the documents specified in either case the Vendor shall be deemed to have covenanted AND HEREBY COVENANTS that he has the right to transfer property in the Yacht and that the same is free from all encumbrances, debts, liens and the like except such encumbrances and liabilities for duties, taxes, debts, liens and the like as are the responsibility of the Purchaser under Clauses 4 and 8.

Free Access after Completion

7.4 On completion, the Vendor shall ensure that the Yacht is available for collection by the Purchaser and that free access by the Purchaser together with all necessary haulage equipment is permitted at no additional cost to the Purchaser.

Rescission of Agreement

8.1 In the event of rescission of this agreement by the Purchaser he shall, at his own expense, reinstate the Yacht to the condition and position in which he found her, and shall pay all boatyard and surveyor's charges for this work.

Return of deposit

8.2 The Vendor shall thereupon return the Deposit to the Purchaser without deduction and without interest save that he shall be entitled to retain such part of the Deposit as shall be necessary to defray any boatyard or surveyor's charges not paid by the Purchaser.
Neither party shall thereafter have any claim against the other under this agreement.

Warranties

9. The Vendor being a person not selling the Yacht in the course of a business, and the Purchaser being at liberty to inspect the Yacht and satisfy himself as to her condition and specification, all express or implied warranties or conditions, statutory or otherwise, are hereby excluded and the Yacht, her outfit, gear and equipment shall be taken with all defects and faults of description without any allowance or abatement whatsoever.

Risk

10. Until the Yacht has been accepted or shall be deemed to have been accepted by the Purchaser she shall be at the risk of the Vendor who shall make good all damage sustained by her before the date of acceptance. If the Yacht be lost or becomes a constructive total loss before such acceptance, this agreement shall be null and void except that the Purchaser will be liable for the cost of all work authorised by him under Clauses 4 and 8 and undertaken before such loss took place and the Deposit shall be returned to the Purchaser without interest but less any deduction made under Clauses 4 and 8 and otherwise without deduction and the Purchaser shall have no claim against the Vendor for damages or otherwise. After acceptance the Yacht shall in all respects be at the risk of the Purchaser.

    Notwithstanding the provisions of this clause the ownership of the Yacht will not vest in the Purchaser until payment of the balance of the Purchase Price in accordance with Clause 7 even though the Purchaser may have insured his risk under the provisions of this clause.

Default by Purchaser

11.1 Should the Purchaser fail to pay the balance of the Purchase Price in accordance with Clause 7, the Vendor may give notice in writing to the Purchaser requiring him to complete the purchase within fourteen days of the service of such notice.

    If the Purchaser fails to comply with the notice then the Vendor may re-sell the Yacht by public auction or private treaty and any deposit paid shall thereupon be forfeit without prejudice to the Vendor's right to claim from the Purchaser the amount of any loss on re-sale together with all his reasonable costs and expenses, due allowance being made for any forfeited deposit. On the expiry of the said notice the Yacht shall be at the Vendor's risk.

Default by Vendor

11.2 If the Vendor shall default in the execution of his part of the contract the Purchaser shall, without prejudice to any other rights he may have hereunder, be entitled to the return of the Deposit.

Unless such default by the Vendor shall have arisen from events over which the Vendor had no control, the Vendor shall pay interest upon the amount of the Deposit for the period during which he has held it at the rate of 4% per annum above finance house base rate, together with compensation for any loss which the Purchaser may have sustained as a result of the Vendor's default.

Arbitration

12. All disputes that cannot be resolved between the Parties and which arise out of or in connection with this agreement shall be submitted to a single arbitrator to be appointed, in default of agreement, by the Chairman of the Council of the RYA and the provisions of the Arbitration Act 1950 (as amended) shall apply.

Notices

13. Any notice under this agreement shall be in writing and any notice to the Purchaser or Vendor shall be sufficiently served if delivered to him personally or posted by recorded delivery to his last known address. Any notice posted shall be deemed to have been received forty eight hours after the time of posting and any notice given in any other manner shall be deemed to have been received at the time when, in the ordinary course of post, it may be expected to have been received.

Jurisdiction

14. This agreement shall be construed according to and governed by the Law of England (or of Scotland if the Vendor's address shall be in that country) and the Parties hereby submit to the jurisdiction of the Courts of the same countries.

Marginal notes

15. The construction of this agreement is not to be affected by any marginal notes.

Rights under contract or statute

16. This agreement forms the entire agreement between the Parties unless otherwise specifically agreed in writing between them.

SIGNED BY THE VENDOR

In the presence of :

SIGNED BY THE PURCHASER

In the presence of :

APPENDIX 4

AGREEMENT FOR THE BAREBOAT CHARTER OF A PLEASURE CRAFT

AN AGREEMENT made the day of 19
BETWEEN :
of ("the Owner")
and
of ("the Hirer")
In respect of the charter of the UN/REGISTERED PLEASURE CRAFT
Name :
Description :-
including all equipment machinery and gear on board ("the Yacht") and any specific inventory attached hereto initialled by both parties and forming part of this agreement.

DEFINITIONS

Charter Period	:	from hours on 19 to hours on 19
Cruising Limits	:	the area bounded by
Charter Fee	:	the sum of £
Advance Payment	:	the sum of £
Balance of Charter Fee	:	the sum of £
Security Deposit	:	the sum of £
Owner and Hirer	:	shall include the persons named above and their respective successors in title.

WHEREBY IT IS AGREED AS FOLLOWS :-

1. **Charter and advance payment**
   Agreement to let
   The Owner shall let and the Hirer shall charter the Yacht for the Charter Period for the Charter Fee. The Advance Payment shall be paid to the Owner on the signing of this agreement. The Balance of the Charter Fee, and the Security Deposit, shall be paid to the Owner in cash or banker's draft at least fourteen days before the start of the Charter Period.

2. **Security deposit**
   The Hirer shall pay the Security Deposit to the Owner as security against the Yacht not being returned in good condition

and towards any loss of or damage to the Yacht occurring during the Charter Period which is the responsibility of the Hirer under Clause 5.3 and against any loss or damage suffered by the Owner due to any breach of this agreement by the Hirer but without prejudice to any claim over and above the Security Deposit which the Owner may have.
The Security Deposit or any balance remaining shall be returned to the Hirer within fourteen days after re-delivery of the Yacht to the Owner or, in the case of dispute, upon the determination of that dispute.

3. **Delivery of yacht**

3.1 Before the start of the Charter Period the Hirer shall have the opportunity to inspect the Yacht in company with the Owner or his agent for the purpose of ensuring that the Yacht and its equipment are in proper working order and further shall have the right to insist on a trial of at least one hour's duration. Acceptance of the Yacht shall imply (prima facie) that the Yacht is in good order.

Hirer's Competence

Likewise the Owner shall have the right to insist that the Hirer and at least one member of his party accompany the Owner for trials to establish to the satisfaction of the Owner their ability to handle the Yacht unattended in the Cruising Limits.

3.2 **Hirer's failure to accept delivery**

If the Hirer shall fail to accept delivery of the Yacht within forty eight hours from the start of the Charter Period and shall not have notified the Owner of his intention to accept delivery later during the Charter Period, then the Owner shall be at liberty to treat this agreement as determined. The Owner's rights upon termination shall be set out in Clause 7.1 the Hirer shall, however, be given credit for any sum recovered by the Owner if he succeeds in re-letting the Yacht in accordance with the conditions set out in Clause 7.3.

4. **Obligations of the owner**

The Owner hereby UNDERTAKES as follows:

4.1 **Owner's duty on hand-over of Yacht**

To use his best endeavours to hand over the Yacht to the Hirer at the start of the Charter Period in full commission, fully bunkered (subject to Clause 4.3) in good condition and with all the necessary gear and equipment, including any items specified in the inventory and any tools and equipment necessary for minor foreseeable repairs. The Owner does not warrant the fitness of the Yacht in all conditions of weather for any particular cruise or passage within the Cruising Limits.

4.2 **Refund for delay or non-delivery**
To use his best endeavours to deliver the Yacht to the Hirer at the agreed time and place. If for any cause the Yacht shall not be so delivered then, subject to Clause 3.2, a pro rata refund shall be made to the Hirer for each complete twelve hours' delay. If the delay should exceed forty eight hours, this agreement shall become null and void and the Owner shall return to the Hirer the Advance Payment, the proportion of the Charter Fee already paid and the Security Deposit in full, but without further liability for either party to pay compensation to the other.

4.3 **Fuelling**
To use his best endeavours to hand over the Yacht at the start of the Charter Period in a fully bunkered condition, but if he is unable to do so then he shall agree with the Hirer upon handover the levels of usable fuel, lubricating oil, water and other similar stores.

4.4 **Provision of documentation**
To obtain and provide any necessary documentation for the Yacht in accordance with the regulations for the time being in force under the Customs and Excise or other Acts and any amending statute, and to assist the Hirer to ensure that the Yacht is provided with the necessary ship's papers.

5. **Obligations of the hirer**
In addition to the obligations of the Hirer in respect of insurance in Clause 6 the Hirer UNDERTAKES as follows :

5.1 **Take-over of stores etc.**
If at the commencement of the Charter Period the Yacht is handed over in a fully bunkered condition, to return the Yacht at the end of the Charter in the same condition. In other circumstances it shall be the Owner's obligation to agree with the Hirer the present levels of all usable fuel, lubricating oil, water and other similar consumable stores at the commencement of the Charter and the Hirer shall be responsible for ensuring that the Yacht is returned at the end of the Charter similarly bunkered. In the event that the Hirer does not fulfil this obligation a difference in levels shall be agreed between the Owner and the Hirer at the end of the Charter and the cost of the difference shall be deducted from the Security Deposit.

5.2 **Payment of running expenses**
To pay for all running expenses during the Charter Period, including the cost of charts (if not supplied), food, laundry charges, water, fuel, bills of health, harbour dues, port dues, pilotage, victuals and provisions for himself and his party.

5.3 **Reparation for loss or damage**
With the exception of loss or damage arising from latent defects or from fair wear and tear, to make good all loss of or damage to any stores, gear, equipment or furnishings of every kind belonging to the Yacht caused during the Charter Period which is not recoverable under the Insurance effected by the Owner as well as any loss or damage arising after the Charter Period but attributable to any act or default of the Hirer or any member of his party.

5.4 **Hirer's duty to report accidents or damage**
To report to the Owner (and, where applicable to the insurers) as soon as possible any event likely to give rise to a claim under the insurance and any other accident, damage or failure of or to the Yacht, and to comply with any reasonable instructions given to him by the Owner of the insurers.
The Hirer shall use his best endeavours to obtain the approval of the Owner, and shall obtain a written estimate for any work likely to cost over £50, before putting any repairs in hand.

5.5 **Agreement not to sub-let**
Not to lend, sub-let or otherwise part with control of the Yacht.

5.6 **Restriction of use**
Not to use the Yacht for any purpose other than private pleasure cruising for himself, his crew and his guests, not to race the Yacht without the prior consent of the Owner. The Hirer further undertakes not to tow any dinghy but to lash it on deck.

5.7 **Maximum number of persons on board**
To limit the number of his party to not more than the number of berths on the Yacht unless the Owner grants permission for a greater number.

5.8 **Cruising Limits**
Not to take the Yacht outside the Cruising Limits.

5.9 **Unlawful acts**
Not knowingly or recklessly to permit to be done or to do or fail to do any act which may render void the Owner's policy of insurance or result in the forfeiture of the Yacht.

5.10 **Indemnity by Hirer in cases where yacht insurance becomes void**
If the insurance policy of the Yacht shall be rendered void or the policy monies withheld in whole or in part by reason of any act or default of the Hirer or any member of his party, the Hirer hereby agrees to indemnify the Owner against any loss consequent upon such act or default.

5.11 **Duty of care**
To be fully responsible for the safety and security of the Yacht at all times during the Charter Period. Unless the Yacht is

moored or anchored in a harbour, marina or similar location, he further undertakes that the Yacht shall at no time be left unattended and at least one member of the party shall remain on board in such circumstances.

5.12 **Observation of regulations**
To observe all regulations of Customs, Port, Harbour or other Authorities to which the Yacht becomes subject.

5.13 **No animals on board**
At no time during the Charter Period to allow any animals on board the Yacht.

5.14 **Customs clearance**
To ensure that the Yacht is properly cleared by British Customs on leaving for and returning from abroad.

6. **Insurance and liabilities**

6.1 **Yacht insurance**
The Owner shall insure the Yacht for its full market value against fire and all the usual marine and collision risks with protection and indemnity cover of at least £1,000,000 (but not so as to cover the first £50.00 of any claim, or damage to sails unless caused by a dismasting or collision). The Owner also undertakes to inform the appropriate broker or underwriter that the Yacht is on charter to the Hirer for the Charter Period. The Owner will provide for the Hirer on request a copy of the policy or certificate and shall ensure that the Hirer is covered under the policy or certificate for the same risks as the Owner himself.

6.2 The Owner shall not, however, be liable for any personal injury, or any loss of, or damage to, the personal property of the Hirer or any member of his party, or any other person invited aboard the Yacht by the Hirer during the Charter Period.

6.3 Should major damage occur to the Yacht during the Charter Period so as to involve a claim on the policy of insurance as described in Clause 6.1 or should a major breakdown of the gear or machinery occur of a nature to make the Yacht unseaworthy, a pro rata refund will be made for the period during which the Yacht was unseaworthy, PROVIDED ALWAYS that neither the Hirer nor any member of his party caused or contributed to the damage or breakdown.

6.4 Notwithstanding anything in this agreement the Hirer shall not be entitled to claim from the Owner any other compensation in respect of damage or breakdown or of any consequential loss however caused.

6.5 If the Yacht shall become an actual or constructive total loss during the Charter Period then provided that the insurance of the Yacht has not been rendered void or the policy monies withheld in whole or in part by reason of any act or default of the Hirer or any member of his party this agreement shall terminate and the Security Deposit and the pro rata proportion of the Charter Fee shall be repaid to the Hirer.

7. **Termination of agreement**

7.1 **Hirer's failure to pay or comply with terms of agreement**
If any payment due under this agreement is not made on or by the appointed day, or if the Hirer fails to comply with any other provision in this agreement, the Owner may forthwith terminate this agreement and resume possession of the Yacht, but without prejudice to the right of the Owner to recover any unpaid part of the Charter Fee and damages in respect of any breach of this agreement by the Hirer.

7.2 **Notice of withdrawal more than two months prior to commencement of Charter period**
If the Hirer gives written notice to the Owner more than two calendar months before the start of the Charter Period that the Yacht will not be required, no liability for the Balance of the Charter Fee will remain (and if it and/or the Security Deposit have already been paid then it and/or they shall be refunded by the Owner to the Hirer), but the Advance Payment shall be forfeit except that 50% will be refunded if the Owner re-lets the yacht for the Charter Period at the same or a greater charter fee. In such circumstances the Owner agrees to use his best endeavours to re-let the Yacht.

7.3 **Notice of withdrawal within two months of commencement of Charter period**
If the Hirer gives notice to the Owner within two calendar months before the start of the Charter Period that the Yacht will not be required, then the Owner will use his best endeavours to re-let the Yacht and the following provisions shall apply :

7.3.1 If the Owner is unable to re-let the Yacht, then the Hirer remains fully liable for all payments due under this agreement;

7.3.2 If the Owner is able to do so at the same or a greater charter fee, then the Hirer's liability shall be limited to 50% of the Advance Payment;

7.3.3 If the Owner is only able to do so at less than the Charter Fee, then the Hirer will be liable for the difference between the net sum which the Owner receives and the payments due under this agreement.

8. **Re-delivery of the yacht**

8.1 **Hirer's responsibility upon re-delivery**

The Hirer will re-deliver the Yacht to the Owner free of indebtedness at the end of the Charter Period in as good, clean and tidy condition as when delivered to the Hirer (fair wear and tear excepted), at the Yacht's base or other mutually convenient place to be notified to the Hirer.

8.2 **Penalty for late return of yacht**

If the Hirer shall fail to re-deliver the Yacht at the time and place agreed, he shall be liable to pay to the owner the sum of £ [   ] for every day or part of a day by which re-delivery is delayed unless the delay is caused by the operation of a peril covered by the terms of the policy or certificate of insurance referred to in clause 6.1 hereof or by such damage to, or failure of, the Yacht as may have been reported to the Owner under Clause 5.4

9. **Settlement of disputes**

In the event of any dispute arising out of this agreement such shall be referred to a sole arbitrator whose decision shall be final. If the parties are unable to agree on the nomination of an arbitrator then he shall be nominated by the Chairman of the Council of the RYA.

10. **Law**

This agreement shall be governed by English Law.

11. **Marginal notes**

The Explanatory marginal notes shall not affect the meaning of nor form part of this agreement.

SIGNED BY THE OWNER

in the presence of :

SIGNED BY THE HIRER

in the presence of :

APPENDIX 5

AGREEMENT FOR THE SYNDICATE OWNERSHIP OF A YACHT

AN AGREEMENT made the day of 19
BETWEEN of
(the first owner)

and of
(the second owner)

The owners include their respective successors in title and shall hereinafter be collectively referred to as the Parties".
WHEREAS the Parties wish to enter into an agreement to share the management and use of the yacht (the Yacht)

[and WHEREAS the first owner is the present owner of the Yacht]

[and WHEREAS the second owner has by a prior contract purchased from the first owner /64ths of the Yacht]

[and WHEREAS the Parties have jointly and severally purchased the Yacht in the following shares :
the first owner purchasing /64ths
the second owner purchasing /64ths

and WHEREAS the parties have jointly and severally entered into an agreement with [ ] (the Mortgage Company)].

NOW IT IS HEREBY MUTUALLY AGREED between the Parties as follows :

1. **Joint Bank Account**
   The first owner shall forthwith open a [Bank/Building Society] account (the Account") in the names of the Parties into which the Parties shall upon the [ ] day of [ ] in each year transfer the amount of £[ ] until six months after the termination of this agreement in accordance with Clause 5.

2. **Withdrawals and Contributions from/to account**
   The first [and second] owner/s shall have power[jointly/separately] to draw monies from the Account for the sole purpose of the maintenance and management of the Yacht as

[he/they] shall in their absolute discretion think fit and shall have power to call for further and necessary contributions in equal shares from [the second owner/each other] subject always to the safeguards in Clause 4.7 and to the general law affecting principal and agent.

3. **Casual disbursements**
Any disbursement, payment or account discharged by one owner on behalf of the other and of the general management of the yacht shall from time to time as convenient but certainly once annually be reported to the other owner and each owner jointly and severally agrees to contribute one half of such disbursements, payments or accounts upon proper documentation in the form of receipts, etc. being presented as evidence of payment.

4. **Management responsibilities**
The first owner shall have the following powers, duties and responsibilities :

4.1 to make day-to-day decisions for the general management of the Yacht;
4.2 to make (after consultation with the second owner) any arrangement for the purchase of capital equipment such as sails, engines etc. as may be necessary and for any agreement to charter the Yacht;
4.3 to insure the Yacht, her apparel, fittings etc. against the usual risks either at Lloyds or with an insurance company or association;
4.4 to employ any yard, sail-loft, brokers or agents on their usual terms of business and to transact any necessary business in relation to the Yacht;
4.5 to make, adjust, apportion or settle at his discretion any salvage, damage, average or other claims in favour of or against the Yacht or to refer the same to arbitration;
4.6 to take such steps as may be necessary to defend proceedings, accept service or arrange finance relating to the Yacht;
4.7 as soon as reasonably practicable after the [ ] day of [ ] in each year to render to the second owner accounts paid together with the Account statements as evidence of payment, and on request to produce all vouchers, books or other documents and papers relating to the management of the Account and of the Yacht.

5. **Termination of agreement**
If either of the Parties has reasonable cause or desire to terminate this agreement, he may, by individual notice in

writing to the other party, indicate his desire to terminate. Such termination shall take place within six months after the delivery of such notice in writing. Upon such notice in writing being delivered, the other party shall take such steps as may be necessary to secure the execution of a proper release and indemnity against all liabilities contracted by the determining party and shall arrange to purchase the share of the determining party at a fair market price or alternatively obtain agreement by another to take on the share of the determining party. Likewise, the determining party hereby agrees to defray or settle all his share of the disbursements, payments or accounts for the Yacht up to and including the date of actual termination as agreed between the Parties which for the avoidance of doubt may be any date within six months of the individual notice in writing being received by the other party.

If a dispute arises as to the price to be paid to the determining party for his share then a valuation shall be obtained from a recognised yacht broker and in default of agreement then the entirety of the Yacht shall be publicly advertised for sale with notice of time and place for sale being given to both Parties and she shall be sold. Each of the Parties on receiving his share of the purchase money shall execute the necessary Bill of Sale of his share in the Yacht to the purchaser and deliver up possession of the Yacht. The costs of such sale shall be paid by the Parties according to their respective shares.

6. Where it is agreed to terminate this agreement and the Parties have mutually agreed to sell the Yacht, it shall then be sold either by private treaty at such price as the Parties may agree or, in default of such agreement, by public auction subject to such conditions as are usual on the sale of such yachts. Each of the Parties shall be at liberty to bid for and purchase the Yacht at any such public auction, or to purchase the Yacht outright for the price advertised for sale by private treaty.

7.1 **Regular payment of mortgage etc.**

In the case of a mortgage or hire purchase agreement being in operation each owner jointly and severally agrees to pay his monthly or other contribution to defray the costs of such mortgage or hire purchase agreement into the Account in accordance with Clause 1 until the date of determination agreed in accordance with Clause 5.

7.2 **Final settlement of mortgage**

In the event of the sale of the Yacht, each owner jointly and severally agrees with the other to defray from his share of the sale price his share of the mortgage or hire debt purchase agreement entered into with the Mortgage Company.

8. **Arbitration**
If any dispute, difference or question arises between the Parties relating to the rights, duties or obligations of either of them, including (without prejudice to the generality hereof) any dispute, difference or question whether the owners have, in fact, properly and satisfactorily carried out their obligations under this agreement, the same shall be referred to arbitration by a single arbitrator to be agreed upon by the Parties or, failing such agreement, appointed by the Secretary-General of the RYA. This shall be deemed to be a submission to arbitration within the Arbitration Act 1950.

9. Any notice under this agreement shall be in writing and shall be sufficiently served if delivered personally or posted to the last known postal address in Great Britain or Ireland of either of the Parties.

IN WITNESS whereof this agreement has been signed by the Parties the day and year first above written

SIGNED BY THE FIRST OWNER

in the presence of :

SIGNED BY THE SECOND OWNER

in the presence of :

NOTES

NOTES

NOTES